BEGINNINGS
How 14 Poets Got Their Start

Interviews

by Derek Alger

BEGINNINGS
How 14 Poets Got Their Start

Interviews

by Derek Alger

Beginnings: How 14 Poets Got Their Start

Copyright © 2015
Each copyright is retained by the author

All rights reserved. No part of this book may be used or reproduced in any manner whatsoever without written permission from the copyright holder, except in the case of short quotations embodied in critical articles or reviews.

ISBN: ISBN: 978-0-9862146-2-2

Cover photograph: 123rf.com

Serving House Books logo by Barry Lereng Wilmont

Published by Serving House Books, LLC
Copenhagen, Denmark and Florham Park, NJ

www.servinghousebooks.com

Member of The Independent Book Publishers Association

First Serving House Books edition 2015

Remembering Derek Alger

Derek Alger cared very much about writers, proud that he enjoyed friendships with so many. During conversations it was apparent that he was surprised to be in such company, as if he didn't quite belong. But he certainly did, more than worthy in his roles as editor, fiction writer, memoirist, and interviewer.

He was an especially gifted interviewer, seemingly in the background, asking questions in only a few sentences. Yet those questions reveal that he had prepared carefully, fully informed about the life and work of the writer, and able to elicit insightful and informative responses.

Derek had published (primarily in *PIF Magazine*) more than one hundred interviews, which we had been encouraging him to publish in collections like this one. He finally agreed, going though his files and choosing contents one at a time, starting with poets. He had compiled these fourteen by the time of his final illness and untimely death. Writers' responses to the shock of his loss revealed that they valued him as much as he did them.

As an interviewer, Derek took a unique approach. He wanted to know how people discovered they were writers and, once they did, how they advanced their careers. His interest was in the writer as a person who realized and fulfilled his or her talent.

Each of the interviews in this collection tells the story of a poet's career, starting with origins that in many cases overcame unlikely beginnings and went on to fortunate educations with inspiring teachers who often became friends and colleagues, and in at least one case a spouse. Then onto publication, books, awards, and, for the majority, their own teaching careers to share their gifts with others in emulation of their own mentors. Each interview is followed by samples of the poet's work. Readers will have an opportunity to appreciate and admire the fourteen poets as people and as artists.

We all—those interviewed and those of us at Serving House Books—consider this book a tribute to Derek Alger for his enthusiastic furtherance of the arts and literature in so many venues and for his own rich human qualities. We miss him and all the future achievements we will never see, but we will remember his as a life devoted to literature and literary colleagues.

—Walter Cummins

Contents

Clifford Brooks III / 9

Travis Cebula / 18

Alfred Corn / 40

Robert Dana / 54

Ani Gjika / 61

Kelle Groom / 71

Julie Kane / 84

Amy King / 97

Gloria Mindock / 108

Mark Statman / 116

William Trowbridge / 128

Pamela Uschuk / 140

Nancy White / 159

Bill Yarrow / 168

Clifford Brooks III

Charles Clifford Brooks III, a true poet from the Georgia landscape, has been published in *The Dead Mule, Eclectica, Gloom Cupboard, Red Fez, Zygote in My Coffee,* and *The Cartier Street Review*, just to name some.

His recent poetry collection, *The Draw of Broken Eyes and Whirling Metaphysics*, published by John Gosslee Books, was greeted with great critical acclaim.

photo by Matthew Polsfuss

Brooks lives in Athens, Georgia, and has been featured on the "Joe Milford Poetry Show" and vox poetica's "15 Minutes of Poetry." He is currently on the road, seeing what he can and doing what he can, and of course, continuing to write emotionally moving poetry.

Derek Alger: With the publication of your first poetry collection, The Draw of Broken Eyes and Whirling Metaphysics, *it looks like you're getting some well deserved recognition.*

Clifford Brooks: Being nominated for the Pulitzer and Georgia Author of the Year has already exceeded my expectations concerning creative writing in poetry. It's still surreal for me to think about. I have been writing since the fifth grade, but, until my early 30's, that writing concentrated on prose. I won contests with fiction and non-fiction and wrote poetry when necessary to woo a young lady. I am grateful to John Gosslee Books for seeing the promise in my verse, and getting behind my double-volume collection. It's always been my highest hope to grow into an established writer.

DA: How did publication come about?

CB: In 2003, a literary agent in New York accepted me as a client. He decided I should pursue publication as a poet. Working with the agent, *Whirling Metaphysics* was edited from a wad of memories into a focused account of a man trying to interpret the world. In 2004-2005, a small publisher showed interest in gaining rights to the work, but, as the current economic recession crippled America's spending habits, both the agent and small press went under.

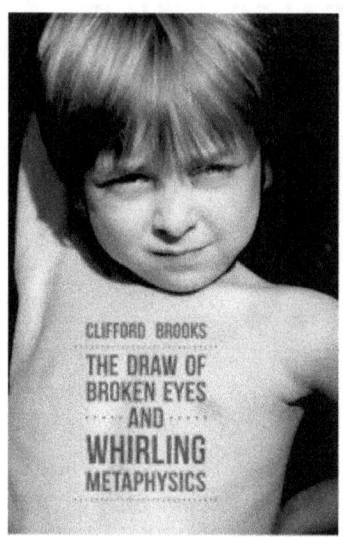

Losing this initial launching point didn't destroy me. I realized that this setback was due to the stock market, not my lack of talent as a poet. Besides that, more pressing matters were on my mind: I was getting a divorce, moving back to Athens, Georgia, leaving a career with social services to write full time, while dealing with morphing Bipolar Disorder symptoms, and new chemical dependency issues. Then, of course, I began the love story with a gorgeously dark heart, from which would come *The Draw of Broken Eyes*.

DA: *Sounds like you definitely had persistence, despite the obstacles.*

CB: In January 2010, I was unexpectedly trapped by an ice storm in my father's home in Watkinsville, Georgia. I decided, in that isolation, that a young lady—the first and only to slow all the internal chaos—needed a love letter to know I would wait. That letter is the central thread of *The Draw of Broken Eyes*. Annmarie Lockhart announced the completion of Broken Eyes on her radio show vox poetica's "15 Minutes of Poetry." After that program, Annmarie introduced me to John Gosslee, the obvious namesake of his press.

In May 2011, John Gosslee Books signed a contract with me for both collections to be published under one cover. After agreeing on the terms of publication, every page was furiously edited and re-edited. By publication date, the book had become my sole obsession. The release date of the collection was April 2012.

DA: You've described your childhood as "idyllic."

CB: I grew up in Crawford, Georgia. Both of my parents were college educated and worked hard to afford a safe, nurturing, and spiritually-sound upbringing for their two sons. I was never told to go outside and play. I was always outside. Nature features prominently in both books because it's always helped me maintain an overall sense of calm. Growing up in the South has its benefits and unique attributes, as does anyone's hometown.

During the day, while both parents worked, my little brother and I were watched by a wonderful black woman named Virginia Smith. Her influence on me runs deep. I went to church with her. I often played with Virginia's children, and they taught me to dance. My father loved Motown, so I grew up hearing it, which rounded out my spiritual connection to music.

Behind my house were a lake, gulley, a slow stream, and trees that seemed to hug my childhood's playground. I never took a shine to school. I was expected to make good grades, and I did pretty well with that. I was undoubtedly more Huck Finn than Tom Sawyer. I got into my share of "mischief," but a healthy serving of discipline from my mom and dad kept it in check.

DA: You have close family ties and roots to Georgia?

CB: Georgia is where you find all my family ties. I love to travel; I feel in my bones a need for an extended visit to Europe, or somewhere a little sunnier in the winter months, but Georgia will always be "home." You either love or hate the South. I cherish this land, but understand why others don't—I simply don't agree with them. The mountains, coastline, and humid spaces in-between are in my bones and blood. I am named after my grandfather and father: Charles Clifford Brooks III.

Since I moved back to Athens, my father and I spend every Sunday maintaining the family plantation house in Lexington, Georgia. It's all about bloodlines and appreciation of one's history. When it rains on Sunday, dad and I go inside and work on preserving newspaper articles from decades past about our ancestors. In reading the meticulously-kept documentation concerning our family tree, I come to understand my French ancestors, whose enterprising ideals prompted their passage to America. Moreover, I acknowledge the American politicians, businessmen, artists, and scoundrels (everyone admires a good rogue) who give me an idea of what I can become.

My mother's people are in the Rome, Georgia area, where I graduated from Shorter College. I spent my senior year living with my Granny (my mother's mother). To this day, she is my favorite roommate—ever. My mother's family is filled to the brim with hardworking, brilliant, and eccentric characters. I am a storyteller ahead of all else. I get that talent and passion from both sides of my family, with both sides adding to the yarns I spin in ink.

DA: Sounds like your parents instilled you with the right values.

CB: What both of my parents fostered in me was an open mind and social tolerance. Color lines blurred for me from birth. That's never changed. I do not state that to announce a moral superiority on my part. I feel I confine that rare experience from childhood when I say, from Virginia, I still find personal strength from gospel music, love God for all His love and not fear of His wrath. Actually, that feeling about God marries in with my parents, too. In my entire young life, I never had to be convinced of God's existence. I felt it on an atomic level. I didn't really dig Sunday School because it was too damned early, but I never remember being "taught" the concept of God. It made sense. It still does.

Two ministers are also partly responsible for this ease of belief. Reverends George Hall and Charles Walker were both Biblical scholars who beamed with compassion, always emphasizing God's infinite love. I never experienced "hellfire and brimstone" preaching. I would rather have my hand slammed in a car door than sit through a sermon of fear.

DA: If I ever want a tour of Georgia I'll know where to go.

CB: In North Georgia, there are rolling mountains that seep into the Appalachians. Middle Georgia levels out into a delicate, straight line that meets Florida swampland. Driving all over the state as a college student solidified these regions in my writing life. On my travels, I took note of the elderly couple dining in a roadside diner, a woman sitting alone in a truck outside a hardware store, and conversations between friends at a gas station. The cliché, "Write what you know" is the first rule of any creative writing. I never "tried" to be a Southern poet. Being Southern is all I know. I don't write poetry to sway people's racial tolerance, religious views, or whom they vote for in the next election. I write what I see every day, how that makes me feel, and the way it influences where I put my faith.

In my extensive walk across these Southern states, I've discovered that New Orleans, Louisiana; Savannah, Georgia; Athens, Georgia; and Charleston, South Carolina all share the same wind, identical Old South voodoo-devotion to Sunday, and a palpable devotion to music—real music. In these cities, there is easy traffic, blues tunes, electric jazz, and a flavor of rock-and-roll that still defines America. We have Elvis Presley, John Lee Hooker, Thelonious Monk, Edgar Allan Poe, Flannery O'Connor, William Faulkner, Eudora Welty, The Allman Brothers, Pat Conroy, and Rick Bragg.

We have no reason to apologize to anyone. Many white Southerners (men especially) have been yoked with "White Guilt," where the racism chronicled in our history isn't the norm of us all. I have never had slaves. I have never controlled anyone. I can barely take care of myself, and failed at caring for a wife—I do not have the wherewithal to have sway over anyone else's life. Southern tradition does not mean "ignorance," or "hate-monger" or "Ku Klux Klan." The tragedy is that generations of Southern Americans have grown to be ashamed of themselves and buy into the propaganda accepted in even mainstream standup comedy. I find it disgusting. I find it false. I find it a tragedy.

I do not glorify Southern tradition. I do not build a case in defense of it. I don't have to.

DA: Your poetry speaks to universal experience and emotion.

CB: Phrases and memories rush into me from everyday, mundane events. Though they all happen in my area of the country, they are also applicable to anyone who's caught "people watching." I constantly scribble in Moleskine notebooks, and sometimes break conversations with friends to record some line I'm afraid I'll forget if not put on paper immediately. My friends are very tolerant cats and kittens. They are the only ones who see the true effects of my Bipolar Disorder, the insomnia, paranoia, as well as the addictions to skirt the inferno of the manic highs and their antithesis—the Nothing. There is a mystery to poetry I hope to never understand where, out of the ephemera, strands of verse find me. I can't explain or pinpoint it. My friends know that about me and thus give me the grace to be a scribbler-of-thought.

During the spring and summer, imagery flows through me in Technicolor. I want to make dark subjects pretty through deceptive rhyme, not to be glib, but to show awful things happen from what seems divine at the start. They are hard lessons learned. I don't preach. I abhor a soapbox. These are poems I picked up from raves in Atlanta, dirt roads that brought me back to Athens, and on a train when I took the eight-hour trek to North Carolina where my first girlfriend lived.

DA: Your poem "A Plantation Myth: Vengeance" is compelling, and evocative in the simplicity of its power, and a great empathy and understanding of others.

CB: That poem is an invented Old South parable. I grew up hearing nearly-forgotten Old South, Uncle Remus-esque moral tales. With "A Plantation Myth," I wanted to keep that vein of storytelling alive. *Song of the South*, a Disney movie built from Uncle Remus, was banned not that long ago. I saw it in the movie theater as a child. The past and its nuances are the kind of metaphysical storytelling that's unavoidable in my creation of written word. I talk about Uncle Remus in my poem "Six Chapters of Swerve."

DA: You took a circuitous route with different geographical stops before graduating from college.

CB: I started college at Campbell University in North Carolina as a Religion major. From there, I moved to Shorter College to pursue a Degree in Education. After, I took classes at a few other schools during the summer, and then took a year off after adopting alcoholism, before going back to Shorter to end with a History/Political Science degree. This degree gave me a taste of everything at a school like Shorter. From Prometheus passing on fire to the advent of our computer, I learned about it all.

DA: I suspect many would be surprised what your first career job was.

CB: Right out of college, I worked for Barnes & Noble in Athens, Georgia. A friend of mine called me two years later about being a juvenile probation officer. He was big in the police, knew that I was good with kids, and that I would put their welfare ahead of accepted policy. After six years as a probation officer, I moved to the Department of Family and Children's Services. Four years after taking on that gig, I realized too much of my soul was being left at the office when I went home to escape. In this job, the epic poem at the end of *Whirling Metaphysics* called "The Gateman's Hymn of Ignoracium" found its source. So many came through court that were incapable of loving their own kids, and used God or money to manipulate the legal system. One day, as I sat as an observer, I thought, "Hell is too good for some people." In that epiphany, I brought my love of Dante into my daily writing life. "The Gateman's Hymn of Ignoracium" was a way to cope with what policy wouldn't practically allow.

DA: You're also known for your perfectionism when it comes to editing.

CB: The hardest part of the publication process, for me, was editing. It made me go line-by-line through every page to make sure my first book, the mother of two books, spoke the exact language I use every day, that it was me without melodrama, and that it was honest to anyone who invested in the book's reading. There are many love poems, but, as much as they speak to the Only Her, something always feels off. She isn't here. At any rate, I still find peace with an impossible affection.

John Gosslee wouldn't let me half-ass any of my poems. He challenged me. I finally divorced myself from the poetry. By the end, I was able to walk away from the pain. In that hollow space left by catharsis, I still have a hard time making deep, emotional connections with other people. Creating my book took a bit of me I've yet to replace.

DA: I see you derive inspiration from Beethoven.

CB: I have three heroes: Dante, Beethoven, and Doc Holliday. All three have their place in my heart. Beethoven, however, is my Father of Music. I found his sound when I was in the eighth grade. It is the most influential music for me to this day.

Published in *Pif Magazine* May 1st, 2013

Poetry by Clifford Brooks III from "Athena Departs"

BAD POEMS

Bad poems are unlucky pennies.

To sell this poem
is like trading dead puppies
for an abortion.
There's no upside.
It is rot and regret.

This is a debate
to the back
of a deaf man's head.
It's bitching
to a grocery bag.

IN THE BEGINNING

there were two callused hearts.

[Early dawn brought distraction, labor,
a lack of luster
pharmaceutical companies adore.
Last night saw black dogs,
heard the gasps of a panicked child,
struck dumb the boisterous voice.]
…
At noon you said:
Get over here and drive me!

I spent hours with you
lost, boozy, knowing you were thinking
of someone else.
We sped in a thoroughbred
until tears were chased behind
the moon.

Gordon, calmest of man's best friends,
took us to the river
by a path of wildflowers
hidden behind a low stone wall.
We sat near a spot turtles stop to sun.
Do you need your little notebook?
[No. No, I don't.]

The supper we shared
was served by a Lebanese man
sporting bad teeth and good Mexican food.
Our new evening got topped off
with tequila and kisses.

You said:
*I like you too much. I don't need to feel
this affectionate blood.
Remember that there are others.*

That's fine, dark-haired frightened one.
My days are a malady,
where I am thrown asunder in time.
I do not know the day.
I am not aware of tomorrow's appointments.

In the face of all evenings
kin to our memory,
I am cognizant of only this encounter,
this football game,
the breath before I leave.

Remember how I said before,
as I do now:
*I've grown beyond wanting
anything
from you.*

Travis Cebula

Travis Cebula resides with his wife and trusty dog in Colorado, where he founded Shadow Mountain Press in 2009. His poems, photographs, essays, and stories have appeared internationally in various print and on-line journals.

He has authored six chapbooks of poetry, including *Blossoms from Nothing*, available in 2014 from E-Ratio Editions, as well as five full-length collections. The most recent of which, *Dangerous Things to Please a Girl*, will be released in 2015 from BlazeVOX Books.

In 2011, Western Michigan University and Charles University in Prague awarded him the Pavel Srut Fellowship for Poetry. In addition to his other teaching, writing, publishing, and editing duties, he is a member of the creative writing faculty at the Left Bank Writer's Retreat in Paris, France.

Derek Alger: You're a true son of Colorado.

Travis Cebula: I was born and raised in Golden, Colorado. A few years ago my wife and I even moved back into the same house that I grew up in—I'm about as close to home as a person can get now. I drive past my old schools every day. My wife works as a physician in the hospital where we were both born. Sometimes, life has a way of circling back around on itself. It's been rewarding to be back, both creatively and personally. I love it here, the mountains and the broad sky, and I think that building some history with a place allows a writer (or any artist) to develop a sense of scale and time that's different from what one might create if one is in motion constantly. I know every stick on this property. I broke a lot of them loose myself. I know where there's an old head of a rake rotting in the weeds. I remember when the trees were planted, and watched them grow grand and tall. There's a pear tree outside the window right now, slowly dying. It's been there as long as I can remember. The willows that I used to climb in as a kid are now all dead and gone, casualties of a local ditch company maintaining its right-of-way. I'm not sure I like the feeling of outliving trees.

This landscape is always changing—all of them do—but at a pace slow enough that you wouldn't be able to tell if you weren't there watching it for years on end. That level of observation requires some stillness. If you watch, I mean really pay attention, while the seasons roll past, I think you develop a sense for the moments that matter, those moments when courses shift a little, and you can train yourself to apply that skill, that judgment, that critical thinking in any environment. You can learn to pick out the important swerves much more quickly. I find this to be particularly important when traveling and visiting new places. In those instances it's hard to piece together time for long observation. I've been lucky a lot in life. I've gotten to see a fair amount of the world. I've known love.

DA: One should never underestimate luck.

TC: I've heard people say it's better to be lucky than good (at least in the context of achievement). My parents worked from home, so I got plenty of attention and informal education when I was little. They both worked really hard to explain natural phenomena and share what they knew of the world with me, in detail—plants, creatures, light, life, art, interactions, etc. My mother is an artist and my father was trained as a wildlife biologist, so you can imagine the range of topics we covered. All of our little conversations reinforced the attentiveness that I mentioned before. Dad would crouch down, rummage through some pine needles, and find a little bug—then explain how it fit in the world around it. What did it eat? What ate it? Why does that matter? It's good to build a little perspective. And their particular line of work didn't hurt in that regard, either.

DA: What sort of work did they do?

TC: Not too long before I was born they started to take over the family business from my maternal grandparents who were preparing to retire. To shorten a long and interesting story a bit (one that's probably going to come out in written form eventually) they converted the garage and basement of our house so they could manufacture glass eyes for taxidermy. The bottom floor of the home was, therefore, completely filled with thousands upon thousands of glass eyes for every animal imaginable, from lions to walruses to owls to fish. Before I was old enough to go to school I spent my days in the workshop with them, either painting, coloring, playing, or building things at a little workbench I inherited from our neighbors when their children got too big to enjoy it. Imagine the ball pit at a Chuck E. Cheese filled with eyes. I immersed myself in those eyes. I continued to do so during summers and holidays as I grew up.

One result of this constant exposure—which, I should be clear, was happening since I was an infant—was that the environment was totally mundane to me. I had no idea how weird it was. It was only when I brought friends over to the house that I was reminded that the situation was a tad odd. I imagine the moment of encountering that tableau of false eyes staring and glistening probably was more profound (and in some cases frightening) for them than it ever was for me. Their facial expressions were unequivocal on that score. I was blasé.

On the other hand, having a mindset wherein a roomful of dead eyes is normal, in no way noteworthy, sets one up for a completely different standard for approaching the strange. I feel like I engage oddities with a more neutral and evaluative stance than I would have otherwise. It's kind of like meeting an old friend. That's useful. And, from a content standpoint, I also can't deny that eyes and sight, with all their attendant perils and potential for error, work their way into my poetry now. It tends to be pretty visual, on the whole.

DA: Do you remember when you first showed an interest in writing.

TC: I remember saying when I was nine that I wanted to be a writer. It was the first non-fantastic thought I had about a career for myself. Which is to say I was old enough to realize I wasn't going to be a fireman, an astronaut, or Batman (not that writing isn't a fantastical way to make a living, in its own way). My parents instilled a desire in me to do something I loved from a very young age—love and happiness are more important than money, they would say. And, for better or worse, I took the advice to heart. It ended up affecting pretty much every career plan I've ever had.

DA: *Your parents offered wise advice.*

TC: It takes a little time to figure out what you love. Take reading books, for example. If you've ever wondered how to get a kid interested in reading, tell them they can stay up as late as they want as long as they're reading a book. My parents did. Thus, by age eight I loved to read and have always firmly believed that stories and poems represent deep magic ever since. Or alchemy. So, it made perfect sense to me at that relatively young age that if somebody wanted to read then somebody should increase the amount of reading material in the world… that I might be able contribute to the cause.

DA: *And so you did.*

TC: That was only the first noteworthy instance of following my gut. I enjoyed playing with the English language and learning foreign languages, too, which led to an interest in international relations. An enjoyment of the outdoors led to a study of environmental ethics. A skill at arguing led to considering law school. Still later on, I used my love of eating to become a chef. But, in the end, I came back to writing and that's where I think I will stay. When I'm writing I'm happier and more content than I've ever been at any other job.

My parents were supportive of my scribbling—my mother in particular, being a creative person herself—and they always praised the little poems I wrote for school projects or the surreal stories I would come up with for standardized writing tests (I had no idea that's what I was doing at the time, but looking back on them they were surreal all right). I particularly enjoyed the constraint of Haiku English teachers assigned to me. It required concision, observation, and, in my case, often a twisted sense of humor.

DA: *You had quite an eye opening experience when you were a young teen.*

TC: My dedication to writing as a habit was tested when I was 13. In 1986 I sailed across the Atlantic with my aunt and uncle on their small boat (37 feet long). The duration of the trip necessitated missing two months of my 8th grade year. Somehow my parents convinced my school to let me go, with a few conditions. In order to pass the grade I was given two assignments to take with me: first, some algebra problems (which I wasn't particularly diligent about), and second, to write. I had to keep a detailed journal of what I did and what I saw. I wrote every day—in Spain, in Gibraltar, around the Canary Islands, on Antigua, and yes, in the middle of the ocean. We went for three weeks without seeing land during the main crossing. Writing by hand on a pitching boat during a storm requires some fortitude and a strong stomach, at least. I discovered I had a bit of both, and that both are prerequisites for lasting in this gig. What I wrote that winter was by no means eloquent, but I was attentive and learned a few tricks—the basics of narrative, humor, imagery, and most of all what is a good trigger to build a wider scene. I had to learn how to describe a Barbary ape on a rough wall below a Moorish castle, the crimson silk banners in the wind, the ape in the wind, how the sun hit its tawny fur, the low sun, cold, the glint of it, how the ape's small pink hand reached out as I walked by, how it hoped for candy, like a child, like me, like all of us, how its eyes dripped down a little in disappointment when no food was to be had, how I kept walking, how it disappeared into the dense brush, and how the world was green and shadowed there. How I never saw it again, nor ever would.

My journal needed to be evocative to share my experiences with my classmates. Thirteen-year-olds needed to be able to see what I saw, feel what I felt, or I wouldn't get to move on to 9th grade. I got a feel for writing with something at stake. I still have that notebook on my bedside table. The glue is rotted and the pages are falling out.

DA: And an apprentice writer was born.

TC: By the time I was in high school I was mostly composing poems when I was composing anything on my own time. Poems always have felt more natural to me, more true to my core personality. I have to work pretty hard to type out prose, and I'm still fairly self-conscious about that, but when I'm working naturally what comes out is a poem. Those high school poems were what I think of as the standard romantic crap, big feelings and abstractions, darkness, and all. More or less what I've seen since from students who haven't written too much poetry and have only a few notions of what poetry is really about. There weren't a whole lot of concrete images in those poems; I guess is what I'm saying. And they rhymed, and had meter—both of which I frequently eschew now. But there also was some joy in them, which must have come through for the few people I shared them with—because they told me I was going to be a poet. To be fair, that might have been partly because I was dressed all in black and spent my time brooding in a library. At the time I scoffed, but it seems that some of my friends were prescient. I just wasn't that serious about it. However, luck played a part again. I had a fantastic AP English teacher, Rita Klemm, who instilled a sense of the deep honor and responsibility that authorship entailed. I remember my best friend and I helped her move one weekend, and her house was like the library labyrinth from *The Name of the Rose*. We lifted hundreds of boxes of books that weekend. Libraries are the curse of all movers, and now I'm doing my level best to contribute to the problem by bringing more books into the world. In any case, when I graduated from high school I'd already been thoroughly infected with our peculiar disease. I always did keep writing, regardless of whatever else I happened to be doing in my life.

DA: Where did you go to college?

TC: Well, that's a convoluted path. Lots of places? Maybe it will make a bit more sense if I start out by saying that I always thought of college as being about education rather than training. It's a subtle but important distinction, and not everyone feels that way or is lucky enough to even consider the alternatives. I started out at Claremont McKenna College in California simply because they let me in. I never thought they would, in a million years. They branded themselves as "The Harvard of the West." In retrospect, they probably admitted me merely as a diversity candidate. The school was so privileged in general that a white kid in a leather jacket with part of his head shaved was probably considered a minority.

I spent one year there, majoring in PPE (Politics, Philosophy, and Economics, which I believe was a program they swiped from Oxford or

Cambridge) and International Relations. It turned out that in addition to being privileged, the student body was politically hyper-conservative. That wasn't a good fit for me, and wouldn't have been for most of the other artists I know. On top of that, the education was extremely expensive, and not all that special as far as I could tell. It was mostly a four-year recommendation letter for a cushy job. My roommate spent his summers teaching tennis lessons on Nantucket, if that gives you some idea. He stole my car. I'm sure he works on Wall Street now. Add into that mix the Rodney King riots, not being able to see the mountains because of the smog, a lack of discernible seasons, the fact that it took five hours to drive to the beach on the weekend, and I was pretty much over living in that part of California after a few months. It wasn't a happy place. I knew when I drove away for summer break that I would never be coming back.

DA: Where did you finally land?

TC: I ended up home in Colorado, crashed a party a few days later with a friend and met the girl who would become my wife. I enrolled in a local community college to take core curriculum classes until she graduated from high school and I could figure out what to do next with my life.

DA: And that was?

TC: I've always been a contrarian by nature, so I swore I would never go to Colorado State University—purely because that's where both of my parents went. But I was completely in love with Shannon, my future wife, and that's where she was going. Romantic instinct trumped any misguided principles I might have had. Effectively, I started over academically when I got to Fort Collins. It took me four more years to graduate. Again, I was lucky enough to have a family who valued education and had put aside some money to support my efforts. Which meant that I could take courses that I was interested in rather than needing to choose only ones that led efficiently toward a degree. Thank you for that, family. I followed my gut and took courses in subjects I was curious about—Russian literature, biology, aesthetics, Existentialism, Eastern Philosophy, African politics, etc. Oddly enough, this added up to a PPE by the time I graduated, but with English replacing Economics for the E portion of things. Colorado State was a great experience, and I'm not sure I would have appreciated it as much if I hadn't started out where I did. There was a lot more value to the education than at Claremont or at community college.

My time in philosophy was focused largely on studying environmental ethics, which I supplemented with other courses in environmental policy and natural resource management. Lee Speer was my mentor on environmental topics. He was an irascible man who adored playing devil's advocate just to get students to back up their views on the world. That spoke to me. I also got pretty close with Jane Kneller, who is quite accomplished and knowledgeable about the Enlightenment era (Kant, Hume, Descartes, Spinoza, Berkeley, Locke, Leibniz, among others) and aesthetics. She was my de-facto advisor; since my official one was on sabbatical for three of the years I was there. Both Dr. Speer and Dr. Kneller were generous enough to allow me an open door policy, which is hazardous with undergraduates, and we had a lot of engaging conversations over lunch and outside of class. We mostly talked about ethics, which is always fun for a discussion and also seemed like the most likely sub-field of philosophy to have any bearing on real life, as far as I could tell. The rest was just messing around with critical thinking and logic games. It all had holes a mile wide in it, every bit. Not to mention the academic language and writing style were infuriatingly elitist and obstructive. I hated that and tried to avoid emulating it at every turn, despite much pressure being applied to the contrary.

DA: But all was not philosophy.

TC: When I wasn't studying philosophy, I was working on civil liberties and comparative politics, my interest in travel still driving me to learn about other places. And when I wasn't doing that, I was taking every creative writing workshop that was available. That was when I started getting serious about my poetry—mostly because I finally had some tools to work with and a really good excuse to use them. I didn't write a ton outside of assignments, but I took to the exercises with relish, and put together a strong enough portfolio to win a little writing scholarship for my last year of school. In my poetry workshops I was taught by Bill Tremblay and Laura Mullen, two very different poets, but both wonderful and very supportive in their own ways. I'm still in touch with them, thankfully.

As is always the case, when graduation approached I needed to make some serious decisions about what to do next. Following my previous pattern, I assessed my interests. My love of environmental study and my inherent argumentativeness pointed to a master's degree in environmental ethics followed by law school and a career in environmental law. My love of poetry pointed to an MFA program. At the time, I felt very strongly that if I went straight into grad school in philosophy I would end up in the same boat as Robert Pirsig, who wrote *Zen and Art of Motorcycle Maintenance*, that I just wasn't able to play that game with enough distance any more. And, as far as writing was concerned, I wasn't at all convinced that I was any better than mediocre at that. I felt that there was already more than enough mediocre writing in the world without me adding my little bit to the slush pile.

DA: So what did you do?

TC: After preparing an elaborate meal for some friends (at least by college student standards, bouef bourgignon if I remember correctly) somebody mentioned offhand that I could be a chef. Oh, really? I loved to eat, so I decided to cook. I went to my favorite restaurant in Fort Collins and asked them if they would teach me to cook. They said yes, and I apprenticed there for a year and a half. There has been a lot of conversation about cooking and restaurants over the last few years thanks to the rapid spread of cooking shows on television. A fair amount of that talk has surrounded the abrasive/acerbic personalities of chefs, with Gordon Ramsay carrying the banner of profanity into the airwaves. It's fair to say that whatever happens on TV is nothing compared to what goes on in an actual kitchen.

That first restaurant I worked in had a walk-in cooler whose outside wall looked like a golf ball from the executive chef throwing sauté pans at his underlings. After that level of critique, any feedback I got in writing workshops was tame.

When I left Fort Collins I worked for a while as a surveyor (which, at my level, mostly consisted of walking around outside and hammering various objects into the ground) before starting culinary school. After going through an apprenticeship and a bachelor's degree the associate's level program in culinary arts was pretty easy. I already had my core knowledge courses taken care of with redundancy to spare, so I could focus exclusively on cooking. We learned about cuisine from all over the world, in all different styles, which fit well with my eclectic personality. The most interesting thing I observed was an inherent difference between people from the east coast and people from the west in terms of how they conceptualize space. The difference manifested itself when it came time to present dishes to professors for evaluation: inevitably, a student from the east coast would have all the elements of his or her dish packed as high as they possibly could in the middle of the plate, covering as little of an area as was structurally sound. On the other hand, westerners covered every available surface of the plate like a painting, flat and wide. It was a response to their known environment, I'm sure.

I helped open my first restaurant while I was in school, which won a few awards and accolades, and went on to open another with my brother-in-law, who went to culinary school with me, shortly thereafter. It was an Irish-themed spot called Limerick Irish Kitchen. And yes, we had a thick book of dirty limericks stashed behind the bar. Sadly, it didn't last long.

DA: Another life change came your way?

TC: Not too long after Limerick closed my wife proceeded from medical school into her residency program here in Denver. The selection of residency for medical students is a Byzantine process unlike any I've ever encountered. It's called "The Match," and basically, every medical student in the country applies to the residencies they'd like to attend, they get interviewed, and then rank-order their list of preferences. The programs more or less do the same, and the lists are fed into a big computer that chews them through an algorithm of some sort. Then all the candidates across the country gather at parties on the same day, Match Day, to find out where they'll be living for the next three to seven years. Up until Shannon's Match Day we had no idea if we'd be in Portland, Maine or Portland, Oregon, or get to stay home. It turned out that Denver was as excited about her as she was about it.

DA: A lucky break.

TC: We knew we could stay in our home, which at that time had a lush and happy pear tree with wood ducks waddling around under it in May and September. But medical residency brings other challenges with it, as well. Not the least of which is the schedule, which legally is supposed to be limited to 80 hours a week with mandatory time off, but which, in reality, ends up being more like 90-100 hours per week with several 36 hour shifts thrown in and months without a day off. If you match that up with a chef/restaurateur schedule of 60-80 hours per week on an offset schedule, you'll see there's not too much opportunity for a shared life. Which meant it was time for a change for me, and I felt like the change should be something with a bit more flexibility in it so I'd be able to flow with my wife's schedule. She strongly suggested that I reconsider writing and MFA programs.

DA: You were fortunate to have a wise and supportive wife.

TC: I applied to Naropa University's Jack Kerouac School of Disembodied Poetics, expecting that if I was accepted (which I considered an outside shot at best) I would start the program six months or a year later. About a month after I dropped off my application in the admissions office I received a phone call asking if I'd be interested in starting fall semester, a week and a half later. Just like that, after ten years of not being in a serious academic environment I was in a Master's program. It was more than a little intimidating.

DA: How was Naropa?

TC: Naropa was fantastic for me, but I could see how it might not be for everyone. It was a place where you got out of it what you put in. There was plenty of opportunity to learn, but there was also space to skate along, if that was what you were looking for. I'm very much a self-starter, which is clearly one of the core components of the program. I was able to get a lot out of it. It's also very craft-based, as opposed to teaching or publishing focused (which is a double-edged sword, insofar as there also weren't a whole lot of funding opportunities available). That was important to me, as I take the "F" in MFA very seriously. I only ever intended to be a writer, with publishing or teaching taking a back seat to the art.

My class was an outlier, I've discovered, in that it was packed with incredibly talented writers who were also generous, supportive, loving, and community-oriented. There was no competitive element poisoning the mix, no stabbing fellow students in the bathroom and taking their manuscripts, which means I came out of the program with a community of good friends all over the country. People went out and started journals, presses, taught, opened bookstores, and did all sorts of amazing things that were about more than just their own writing. Look up Marie Larson, JenMarie Macdonald, Jennifer Phelps, Rebecca George, Daniel Dissinger, Kristi Kagy, Richard Schwass, or Adrienne Dodt. They're all doing exciting things, and most of them have books available so you can read more. It was and is a group of true artists and advocates, and I'm overjoyed to be a part of it.

DA: You had some amazing, caring teachers at Naropa.

TC: I was privileged to work with some amazing professors. My first workshop was with Anselm Hollo, who in addition to being witness to some great pieces of poetic history (Black Mountain among them) had a very wry sense of humor and a great ear for poetry. That was my introduction to graduate-level workshops, which I most often describe to non-initiates as a Promethean experience—imagine being chained to a rock and having your liver torn out by giant eagles on a daily basis. You get used to it.

The most important relationship I formed was with my thesis advisor, Elizabeth Robinson. Elizabeth has an uncanny ability to come to writers on their own terms, to interpret their goals in projects, and help guide them to excellence. She's probably the most generous person with her time and energy that I've ever met, a generosity that often gets put to the test with recommendation letter requests, blurbs, and reviews. Occupational hazard. She was also the only professor at Naropa that made an effort to prepare her students for the life of a poet beyond the act of creating poetry. The lucky students who were able to work with her gave a reading, we structured manuscripts, we submitted work to journals, we taught classes, and we wrote reviews of fellow student's manuscripts. Elizabeth's poetry workshop was my first exposure to any of those things, and I wouldn't have had that if not for her. She insisted that we participate in the larger conversation, which has been rewarding ever since.

Last, but not least, I wrote. I wrote and wrote and wrote. The chapbook I put together in Elizabeth's workshop became my first little book of poetry in 2009, *Some Exits*. The creative manuscript portion of my thesis ended up being my first full-length collection of poetry, *Under the Sky They Lit Cities*. *Commence*, a chapbook of haiku I put together to give to my friends at graduation, was the starting point of Shadow Mountain Press. I've published books by eight other authors under the imprint since. I also started writing *Ithaca* while I was there. It was a productive time.

DA: Tell us about the Left Bank Paris Retreat.

TC: The Left Bank Writers Retreat was started in 2010 by Darla Worden and Sarah Suzor. They ran two sessions that summer in Paris, France. I attended the first one, and then came back during the second one to present a short lecture on the importance of food in writing, particularly with regard to Hemingway. The Retreat itself consists of a writing workshop in the morning with exercises and discussion, followed by lunch at a café with a literary connection, and visits in the afternoon to inspiring local sites, including places like Montmartre, Luxembourg Gardens, and the Musée d'Orsay. Paris has no shortage of things to look at. We finished out the week with a visit to Versailles, which I spent bicycling around the extensive gardens behind the palace itself.

I honestly didn't know that much about the Retreat before I went, since it hadn't been held before. I received an email from Sarah saying it would be a great time… I believe Paris, if attainable, is an invaluable stop for an aspiring writer. If you can't find something to write about while you're in that environment, you need to find a new vocation. I had very romantic, and vague, notions about what Paris was like based on a few movies and a few books like *A Moveable Feast* and *Autobiography of Alice B. Toklas*. The mythology of the Lost Generation and the garret Bohemians got its hooks into me, and I made plans to live there for a month in a small apartment. The reality was more than I ever imagined. I write quite a bit under normal circumstances now, but if you give me an excuse, an exercise, or extra motivation that level increases dramatically. In that month I think I produced well over a hundred poems, took a thousand photographs (conservatively), and added another 150 pages of travel journaling. The only book of poetry I had with me was an old

Penguin edition of T.S. Eliot's *Selected Poems*, so that proved to be my lyrical guide through the city. Everywhere I turned there was something to write about; Paris is devoid of "dead air," as far as I can tell. I spent my days just walking around the city, stopping on bridges and street corners—anywhere there was an object I could lean against—to write. Because I was there for an extended period of time I also had the luxury of sitting down and observing the city happening around me, of getting a real feel for the place, its people, and their attitude towards life. It's also validating to be in a place that venerates writers so much, that builds monuments to them.

DA: Sounds like an amazing experience.

TC: I could go on and on about the place, but some of those poems will inevitably be available to read someday, and they speak for themselves. I structured a lot of them as epistolary pieces to Shannon, because that was the first time we'd been apart for an extended period of time since we were married. This poem is an excerpt from a forthcoming book, *Dangerous Things to Please a Girl*, due out in 2015 from BlazeVOX books

"The endless cycle of idea and action"

dear Angel,
    you asked me to explain
    myself, to explain why

I am here. perhaps,
    why the streets are
    so empty and the buildings are

so uniformly grey. perhaps
    you do not remember.
    there are eight stories

to every one, and every one
    begins, "it is Sunday."
    for now it is Sunday and

the cafés are closed.
    four men in chartreuse coveralls
  hose down sidewalks.

cigarettes and stones shine in June almost
    as if it were cold. and it is.
  for once a fireplace makes sense—

from this cracked leather chair I look back
    and forth between the soot on bricks
  and the ink—both feel warmer

than clouds. or water that plummets
    piece by piece. the movement
  of hands over paper provides a bit of

relief, like rubbing tombstones
    in winter, but a less eloquent form
  of friction. less true than a thousand twisted

scarves. all blue. Angel, I am here to write
    this perfect cerulean, yes, and to speak
  only to you of this and these.

these clouds and these leaden roofs
    and geese and their river sliding by the Ile
  Saint Louis like photosynthetic oil.

no one else swims here, and could I
    blame them? even their ghosts would
  freeze, perhaps sink, clean

of such slimy bodies. weeks
    later the bouquinistes along the quays
  would wipe some residue of splashing

rain from their plywood stalls.
    and it would also be green,
  written that way just for you.

DA: And a Left Bank Writers Retreat guy arrived.

TC: In 2012 Darla invited me back ostensibly as a participant, but what turned out to be an extended informal interview for a position as an instructor. I've been an enthusiastic part of the team ever since. I really believe in the program—what students have accomplished there in a short time is really mind-blowing, even people who have never written seriously before. We've had people attend who run the gambit from writing professors to stay-at-home moms, and everything in between. Darla is currently working on a book that lays out some of her exercises and anthologizes a lot of the great stories, poems, and vignettes that have come out of the Retreat over the years.

DA: Was your trip to Paris the inspiration for . . . but for a Brief Interlude at Versailles?

TC: *...but for a Brief Interlude at Versailles* is a chapbook I wrote during that first visit to Versailles. I was sitting in the grass next to the big cross-shaped lagoon in the gardens, surrounded by sculpted hedges, fountains, gilded palaces, a storybook village, etc. The contemporary reality of an exclusive paradise becoming a beautiful park for anyone and everyone felt surreal to me, and I started thinking about surrealism as a whole—specifically where surrealism really got started. It occurred to me that maybe it wasn't Breton and Apollinaire or the usual suspects that get credited for the origins of the Surrealist movement, and that maybe it wasn't even Alfred Jarry or Rimbaud or Verlaine or the Symbolists who really got the ball rolling, or even the Romantics before them. The true origins might have come a lot earlier ... Specifically, I found myself sitting in a place where Louis XIV could go to bed one night, dream, and then wake up the next morning with the resources and the will to make whatever bizarre dream he had that night a physical reality. That was surrealism made concrete, without any conceptual superstructure around it.

    I wanted to put a human face to that, so I chose a child (albeit a royal one) who was thrust into that strange environment to be my mouthpiece: Marie Antoinette. From that decision point on, the manuscript flowed. It was fun imagining conversations she might have had with her husband, Louis XVI, up to and including the French

Revolution. I'm still a little baffled by the decision, but I'm glad I made it.

I've also always been interested in finding ways to incorporate visual art with poetry. In *Some Exits* I included several black and white photographs I took of that landscape. I had a lot of pictures of Versailles and ended up modifying them into illustrations that put literal images in conversation with the poetic ones I was employing. I thought the results were successful, and sent the manuscript to Sarah Suzor, who obviously shares my feelings about Paris (and who I also shared some of the more amusing lines with as I was writing them), and who apparently also spit coffee all over her computer when she read the first page and decided to publish the book on the spot, through her press, Highway 101. I'm grateful for it.

DA: Your early published poetry has been described as "exquisitely spare as the landscapes they contain."

TC: Yeah. Sara Nolan, a dear friend and fellow graduate said that about *Some Exits*, if I remember correctly. I suppose that comes from a synthesis of my sense of place (Colorado and the American southwest are pretty spare and barren places, for the most part) and my strongest poetic influences at the time, which happened to be imagists and objectivists along the order of William Carlos Williams and Lorine Niedecker. I think of Ezra Pound's classic short poem about people in the Metro in Paris. I also found a lot of kinship with the short lines of Robert Creeley. I liked the idea of giving poems a lot of space to breathe on the page. The pacing mirrored my experiences of moving through that environment—both walking and road trips. *Under the Sky They Lit Cities*, some of my observations from growing up in Colorado, is similarly sparse. There are a lot of open spaces in this part of the world. I wonder if she would consider my current work, which moves deeper into cities, quite as spare as those earlier pieces.

DA: Your most recently released collection, One Year in a Paper Cinema, *has a unique premise behind it.*

TC: This is by far the most conceptual and procedural book I've ever attempted. The title refers to 365 separate poems that I wrote over the course of a calendar year, all of them relating to films. I reconstructed one poem each day from the language contained in the primetime movie titles listed in the TV guide of my local newspaper. I decided to organize it by the astronomical calendar rather than Gregorian, just for fun, which means it starts with the summer solstice and proceeds season by season through the year.

To contextualize the project a bit, I guess I should start by saying that I believe humans are essentially narrative creatures—that is to say, our consciousness works in a narrative way. It's how we view, conceptualize, learn about, and organize our world. And by narrative I mean simply that our minds work in terms of a sequence of events, one thing happens after another, be that thing a thought, a perception, or whatever. What else is a story, when you get right down to it, other than sequentiality? To me, that's the most rudimentary form of narrative: one thing just happening after another. I look at a tree; I look at a cloud; then … It all ends up being a function of "next." I can't really focus on everything at once, as much as Picasso or Stein might have wanted me to. And I can't help but assume that other people operate in more or less the same way. Language follows the same rules. One word event happens after another until a sentence, a line, a paragraph, a novel, or a poem forms. So language, at core, is essentially narrative. It might be good narrative, or bad narrative, or strange narrative. But it's still just a sequence of events. So is science, for that matter. So is film. Some poets I know might take umbrage with my stance, poets who are opposed to the supremacy of narrative, but I mean no offense. I just take a very broad view of what narrative is.

DA: You obviously have a love and thorough knowledge of films.

TC: I've always watched a lot of films, and happen to be very close friends with a film critic who I've been going to movies with for the last 30 years or so. He and I have had a lot of conversations over the years about how movies are a peculiarly important part of our society, and how they and other pop-culture reflect the overall mood, values, and concerns of America. Films are one of the most vital vehicles for American mythology. I've always seen titles as being elemental frames for narratives—thus, movie titles would in some way be the elemental frames for our culture's mythology and narrative. The language in movies titles has been hallowed, to a degree, as a designator of what a lot of folks care about. The language gets further refined when movies are selected for re-broadcast on television, and even more refined by being popular (reaching enough of a consensus approval) to be rebroadcast during prime time. I thought it would be interesting to track that language over the course of a year and see what the pure language had to say when removed from its original context. What stories are we telling ourselves over and over without really knowing we're doing it? The poems were of mixed quality, from my perspective. But then, so were the movies I was working from. The poems are sketches of our stories, for good or ill. The timing of the project proved fortuitous, though. Shortly after I finished the manuscript, the newspaper discontinued the little TV guide insert they provided every week, and the material was no longer available. I guess it's now a little piece of time, too. Lots of people I know remember looking through that thing all the time. Now it's gone, and as such has a little ephemeral beauty it never had while it was here. I'm a bit conflicted about feeling nostalgia for something that banal, but there it is.

DA: Your poetry collection, Ithaca: A Life in Four Fragments, *was an ambitious undertaking.*

TC: I have always had a tendency to think of the creative act in terms of parenting, and thus to think of my manuscripts and poems as children. They represent independent lives with rights of their own. You try to raise them well, but eventually you have to stop messing with them and send them out into the world.

At one point in graduate school I was simultaneously reading *Ulysses* and a collection of short stories by Jorge Luis Borges. I came across Borges' short story, "The Circular Ruins," which chronicles the efforts of a magician to dream a son into existence by dreaming of him in detail night after night. I couldn't help thinking this was a much more elegant way of describing how I felt about the process of writing.

At the same time, *Ulysses* and what Joyce does with language in that book fascinated me deeply. I also wondered a lot about the distantly loved and absent character of Milly, Leopold Bloom's daughter. An idea started to coalesce in my mind that combined the two books. I wondered what would happen if bits of language from *Ulysses* were used to dream a daughter (or a country, or a religion, because I saw parallels there). Joyce compresses an entire life (the life of a book, anyway) into a single day. I wanted to let the day breathe back out into an entire lifetime. The result was Ithaca, the fictionalized verse biography of the resulting entity, broken into four fragments. I chose Ithaca both for its reference to Odysseus' home and its ambiguity. Is it a person or a nation-state? I'm still not completely sure myself. However, it is most emotionally compelling for me when I read the book and Ithaca is a person, particularly when she becomes a lonely old woman. I usually tear up a bit when I'm reading from the Confinement section.

The undertaking was ambitious enough to make me uncomfortable now. At the time I was writing the book I was too absorbed in the process to address the issue of "who the hell are you to be messing around with Joyce or Borges, let alone both at the same time?" Certainly, neither one of them needs any help from the likes of me. It's done now, though. The child is effectively launched and in the world.

DA: *You have a co-written book,* After the Fox, *due out next year.*

TC: *After the Fox* is the most fun I've had writing a book, without question. The collaborative process, or at least the way we work it, is like having Christmas presents show up in your email box every day. Sarah Suzor and I did call and response back and forth over the course of a year and a half. One epistolary page responded, turned, and returned to another. Later we remixed the pieces into the sequenced book that's coming out next summer. Working with Sarah is particularly rewarding because we have similar enough poetic sensibilities to maintain a conversation, but disparate enough ones to keep the voices distinct and interesting.

The book follows the pseudo-mythic stories of night and day (in the personae of Nocturnal and Morning) as they chase each other around the world. It started with a simple phrase, "Tally Ho!" which morphed into "after the fox." It seemed like a great metaphor for the grander chase most people find themselves in at one point or another, in one form or another. On the surface the book deals with universal issues of romantic yearning, but under that are a lot of deeper currents about communities, language, life, gender roles, and the fundamental nature of human relationships. What is the importance of a shared history? Is it enough to keep people together? Is wanting enough? What does together mean?

If I had to pick one word to describe the book, it would be "vibrant." Sarah writes the part of Morning, and I inhabit Nocturnal for the purposes of the book. But, in the absence of the names, a reader should be able tell who wrote which parts pretty easily, I think. Sarah's are way better than mine. Her lines are infectious. Her first book, *The Principle Agent*, is still one of the best books of poetry I've ever read. As we were composing the book, I knew I had no hope of competing with the lines she was coming up with, so I felt liberated to not even try. For my part, that removed any notion that we were working in any way other than cooperatively. I suspect she might say the same thing in reverse, if asked. That level of mutual respect is a great place to start from if you're collaborating with someone, I guess. It's been working so far for us, and we're still going.

Sarah and I met originally through Elizabeth Robinson, who we share as a mentor. While were both in graduate school and half a country apart, Elizabeth suggested I submit some work to a journal Sarah was editing in California at OTIS College of Art and Design. She accepted a poem and my cover letter for publication, and we came in contact via email. A few months later she attended a couple of classes at Naropa's Summer Writing Program, where we met in person for the first time. Our paths crossed at some readings in Denver after that, but we didn't really get a chance to spend serious time together until that first year in Paris. We had a lot of great conversations in cafés all over the city, and during the walks to and from them. We just clicked. After that she invited me to read with her at Poet's House in New York, and had the great idea that we should write a little collaborative piece to read together at the event. Those first few pages, set in New York, became *After the Fox*. We've been meeting up to teach, collaborate, and read all over the world ever since. With no end in sight.

DA: What's next on the agenda.

TC: I work best (or at least most) without a set agenda, so I have several projects in various states of completion. On any given day one will call out to me. Sarah and I have a new collaboration in the works about where the world is headed, called *Last Call*. My individual manuscripts are figuratively and literally scattered across the map from New York to Paris and beyond. One was born out of the first man to ever jump off the Empire State Building. Another was born out of three pages of *Tender Buttons* that was boiled in borax for six hours and given to me by fellow poet Julia Cohen. That one's about mothers. Another one's about the future predicting past dreams. They're all quite different from one another, and quite different from any other books I've done before. Creeley's old adage about form being an extension of content is very much at play in my work, and probably always will be. I hate getting in a rut.

I'll keep moving. I'll keep teaching every year in Paris and in Denver when I can, as long as I can. I'll keep stitching chapbooks in between writing poems. I may even try my hand at stories, see where the narratives lead in more depth.

I've learned that if I just keep thousands of glass eyes peeled the world is bound to present something of value. I'll keep making my own glass eyes, my own little poems. They're like the eyes. They're not really alive, I know. But I'll keep trying to dream them as close to life as possible, so that if a person looks at them they'll be able to imagine the life inside.

Published in *Pif Magazine* January 1st, 2014

Alfred Corn

Alfred Corn has published several collections of poetry over the years, including his first collection *All Roads at Once* (1976), *A Call in the Midst of the Crowd: Poems* (1978), *The Various Light* (1980), *Notes from a Child of Paradise (1984)*, and *Tables* (Press 53, 2013). Other collections are *The West Door: Poems* (1988), *Autobiographies: Poems* (1992), *Stake: Selected Poems, 1972-1992*, and *Contradictions: Poems* (2002). In 2014, Barrow Street Press published *Unions* and later in the year  Eyewear Publishers brought out his second novel, titled *Miranda's Book*.

He has also published two collections of critical essays, *The Metamorphoses of Metaphor* (1988) and *Atlas: Selected Essays, 1989-2007* (2008). He was the editor of *Incarnation: Contemporary Writers on the New Testament* (1990) and in 1997 published a novel titled *Part of His Story*, along with *The Poem's Heartbeat: A Manual of Prosody*.

Corn graduated with a B.A. from Emory College, and went on to earn an MA in French from Columbia University. His degree work included spending a year in Paris on a Fulbright Scholarship, and teaching in the French Department at Columbia College.

Fellowships and prizes awarded for his poetry include a Guggenheim fellowship, a grant from the National Endowment for the Arts, an Award in Literature from the Academy and Institute of Arts and Letters, and one from the Academy of American Poets. He also held the Amy Clampitt residency in Lenox, Massachusetts for 2004-2005.
For many years, Corn taught in the Graduate Writing Program of the Columbia University School of the Arts, and has also taught courses and writing workshops at the City University of New York, the University of Cincinnati, Ohio State University, Oklahoma State University, UCLA, Sarah Lawrence, and Yale University to name a few.

In 2007, Corn directed a poetry-writing course at Wroxton College in Oxfordshire, and in 2008, he taught a workshop at the Almassera

Vella in Spain. A Visiting Fellow at Clare Hall, Cambridge in 2012, and was subsequently made a Life Fellow. His play, *Lowell's Bedlam*, opened at Pentameters Theatre in London in 2011.

Derek Alger: I see you continue to be a prolific writer.

Alfred Corn: People often say that, and yet I don't write every day, not even every week. Actually, there have been times when months would pass and not a line would be written. Between *Contradictions* (2002) and the most recent book there was an interval of eleven years when I didn't publish a book, except for a collection of essays that had been written mostly during the 1990s. I wasn't publishing, no, but I was working, at my own pace.

DA: Your eighth poetry collection, Tables, *edited by Pamela Uschuk and William Pitt Root, was published last year. It is a very strong book.*

AC: I'm glad you see it that way. Some of the reviewers described it as a super-sophisticate's book, elegant and worldly. I guess they didn't read the poem about how it feels to suffer bombardment, or the one describing my father's war experience and the aftermath, or the poem about the destruction of the World Trade Towers. I was especially pleased that the book was selected for publication by poets, and these poets in particular, because I'm fully in sympathy with what they stand for.

DA: You have a poetry collection, Unions, *due out later this month.*

AC: That, and my second novel, titled *Miranda's Book*, which will appear in November of this year with Eyewear Publishing in London.

DA: You originally hail from Georgia.

AC: Yes, family origins begin in Virginia and Maryland in the 17th century and then trickle down over time through the Carolinas to Georgia. I haven't lived in my home state since 1961, though. Just made family visits after that. Once I was invited to speak at a conference at the University in Athens, a conference about Georgia poets, but only once. I'm not sure they want to claim me.

DA: Shortly after your birth, your father served in the Army Corps of Engineers in Philippines and then, in 1945, on your birthday, your mother died of complications following a burst appendix. Your father lived to age 81, and you have said you aren't sure he ever fully recovered from your mother's death.

AC: Those kinds of early events are foundational for consciousness. I've done a lot of private speculation about them, and a few poems deal with the subject.

DA: The scholastic world came easy to you.

AC: I put a lot of work into it because in the rather topsy-turvy world of my childhood, learning was something I could actually control, could actually master. Otherwise, I felt more or less powerless. Some testing was done and it appears I had above-average intelligence, anyway, enough to recognize which people had more of it than I did. When I met them, I listened carefully to what they said and tried to learn as much as I could from them.

DA: You learned French at an early age.

AC: I started French language classes in my third and fourth year of high school, after two years of Latin, which helped with French. There was actually a French professor who had come to Valdosta to teach at the local college. Monsieur Jean Guitton, his name was. He made a visit to our class. So I got to hear a native speaker pronounce the language, which helped considerably. He was personally charming and genial, and that added to the attraction of learning his language. Our family never did much traveling, so I felt the lure of other countries strongly, France in particular. I was determined to go there some day and practiced speaking as often as I could in preparation.

DA: You chose to go to Emory University.

AC: I had very high SAT scores and was accepted at Harvard, Yale, Princeton, Columbia, and Emory. I'd won a National Merit Scholarship, which was enough for tuition at Emory but not at the others. It seemed prudent not to go into debt for undergraduate studies, and, besides, I was afraid I'd be too much of a small-town hick to make my way at an Ivy League university. It was a mistake, but on the other hand I did get good instruction at Emory. When time came to go to graduate school, I felt more confident. The same places accepted me, and I chose Columbia because it is located in New York, the cultural center of the U.S.

DA: You were a French major at Emory.

AC: I flattered myself that I would be able to master English literature on my own. But I knew I'd have to have help with French literature. Of course it's not so simple as that, and I'm still trying to learn the English tradition (and making progress!). But also it's the thing I said earlier about hoping to travel and therefore needing to be able to speak another language when that finally happened.

DA: And then, as you already mentioned, on to Columbia University for graduate school.

AC: Yes, and several fellowships guaranteed that it wouldn't cost me anything to attend, assuming I could keep living expenses down to subsistence level. I planned to get a doctorate, teach at a university, and do my own writing during free time. I did all the work for the PhD. except the dissertation. But by then, I'd actually taught French at Columbia College and realized I didn't enjoy teaching grammar and pronunciation to students who weren't especially interested or proficient. I only cared to teach literature, whereas, in a language discipline, you always have to do introductory language courses, even after tenure. Another factor was that around 1970, universities began dropping language requirements for the degree, which meant there were fewer positions available. So I'm not sure I could have had a university career even if I'd wanted one.

DA: Were there teachers you especially liked?

AC: I had the arrogance of most twenty-year-olds, and rather disdained most of my teachers, but I liked P.G. Peckham, who taught Old French, and Michael Riffaterre, who was a critical theorist. He was the director of my MA thesis, a study of the poetry of Henri Michaux. The subject of my PhD. dissertation was to be the influence of Melville on Camus, and the twentieth-century specialist was Leon Roudiez. But as it happens I never finished the dissertation and abandoned my degree. However, I don't regret the work I did in French literature. Another bonus was the Fulbright Fellowship I was awarded, which allowed me to live in Paris for a year. I certainly don't regret that. I knew that I hoped some day to write, but in those years my sights were set more on fiction than on poetry. A few years later the priorities switched.

DA: Your first collection of poetry, All Roads at Once, *received high praise from Harold Bloom.*

AC: Yes, and he went that one better for my second collection, *A Call in the Midst of the Crowd.* I was completely in sympathy with the high value he placed on the Romantic tradition in American poetry, which begins with Emerson and runs through Whitman, Dickinson, Stevens, Crane, and Bishop. On the other hand, he didn't have much use for Eliot, Williams, Moore, Auden, or Robert Lowell, and they were also important to me.

DA: What other writers and poets influenced you?

AC: I've just mentioned several American poets, but I should also speak of European writers, including novelists. Dante, Shakespeare, Cervantes, Milton, Wordsworth, Coleridge, Keats, Byron, Stendhal, Baudelaire, George Eliot, Rimbaud, Tolstoy, Chekhov, Mallarmé, Hardy, Rilke, Yeats, Joyce, Proust, Kafka, and Woolf. Among American novelists, Melville, James, Cather, Faulkner, and Flannery O'Connor. Among Latin Americans, Borges, Neruda, and Octavio Paz.

DA: Tell us a bit about Incarnation: Contemporary Writers on the New Testament.

AC: A friendly associate of mine David Rosenberg had edited a volume dealing with the Jewish Bible, with novelists, poets and non-fiction writers contributing essays about each book. I suggested he do the same for the New Testament. He made the counter-suggestion that I should do it, and I agreed. I knew that there were quite a few writers who were Christian, and so was I in my own unorthodox way. So it promised to be interesting, and was. I thought it would be helpful if biblical writings were rescued from the ranting use that fundamentalists now make of them. Also, you can't understand the Western tradition very well unless you have a good knowledge of its scriptural foundations. It's shocking how many well-educated people have never bothered to read the Bible, though I can understand why they might not want to, having heard it thumped on TV so often.

DA: You are among 23 writers commenting on all books of the New Testament and how it affected their lives and works.

AC: Yes I was. I wrote about Second Corinthians.

DA: What was gist of your essay if you can comment concisely?

AC: My point was this: modern believers find themselves in a position closer to Saint Paul's than to the twelve apostles. Paul (or Saul of Tarsus) never saw or heard Jesus. His knowledge was second hand. He didn't even have the four gospels to read because they weren't assembled till after his death. What he did have was the vision on the road to Damascus. And that is what changed the course of his life. Vision replaced a direct, face-to-face encounter. Modern believers resemble him more than they resemble, say, John or Peter, who actually accompanied Jesus on his mission.

DA: In addition to Reynolds Price, who were some of the other writers?

AC: Very distinguished novelists and poets, including John Updike, Mary Gordon, John Hersey, Anthony Hecht, Grace Schulman, Robert Hass, and Rita Dove.

DA: In Atlas: Selected Essays, 1989-2007, *you were able to demonstrate your varied interests in language, theology, music, theater, and the graphic arts.*

AC: I wouldn't say "demonstrate." I just record my thoughts. But of course those thoughts come from someone with a lot of education, institutional and self-administered. The American tradition is one based on the "Song of Myself." If the self in question happens to have read extensively, traveled extensively, and attended concerts and theater, she or he will inevitably reveal that fact in any honest self-disclosure. I suppose I could try to "talk down" to the audience, but that would be sort of insulting, wouldn't it? When someone speaks to me, and I realize the level of knowledge being imparted is greater than mine, I don't despise the speaker for that. The speaker has paid me the compliment of assuming I can absorb this new knowledge. And that is what I try to do. In the era of the Internet and Wikipedia, there's really no excuse for me not to go and "look it up."

DA: You call yourself "globocentric" and are definitely a polymath. Your essays range from a reminiscence of a journey to Elizabeth Bishops's childhood home; to an exchange of letters you, as a college student, had with Flannery O'Connor, where she writes about the nature of faith; to fresh, as well as informed essays on The Canterbury Tales *and a retrospective consideration of Wordsworth.*

AC: I used the occasion of the bicentenary of Lyrical Ballads to comment on Wordsworth's "retrospective" habits of mind—"emotion recollected in tranquillity" and comparable mental reflexes. To some degree I am retrospective myself, often writing about moments from the proximate or distant past in my own life. I don't know where that propensity comes from. As for being "globocentric," it's an attitude based on the idea that the day of nationalism (and of course chauvinism and nationalistic wars) is over. We have just one world now, Spaceship Earth, and we're all on it together. Anything that happens in one part of the globe affects all other parts. The interconnectivity of the Web is the most convenient symbol of this new global unity, but the same applies to economics, environment, health issues, and artistic culture. In the last century Americans made a big issue out of creating an American aesthetic distinct from Europe's. No doubt one motivation for that initiative was the sense that Europe's achievement was unduplicatable and intimidating. But surely at this point no one doubts the greatness of American art, its achievements in film, music, visual art, dance, and literature. Europe looks to us for inspiration now, so there's really no need to rant at great length about our important place in the scheme of things. We can now afford to draw inspiration from Europe in turn, without the fear of contamination or loss of the democratic spirit.

DA: You received praise because your enthusiasm for Chaucer and Keats is as fresh and inquisitive as for Bishop, Thom Gunn, or Derek Mahon.

AC: Thank you.

DA: The title Atlas *is apt in sense of travel, both physical and abstract.*

AC: Yes, and I don't even mind if someone wants to see it in terms of the figure in Greek mythology who stood on the Atlas mountains and held up Heaven until the gods gave him a break.

DA: You also published a novel, Part of His Story.

AC: I did. It's a narrative of loss and regeneration in the midst of the AIDS crisis, with sectarian violence in Ireland as a secondary concern. It's not autobiographical, but like the narrator I am a writer who has spent a lot of time in London. I didn't have a partner who died of HIV-related illness, but I did have many friends in that situation. My narrator finds a new lover, whose sister is involved in the struggle to wrest Northern Ireland from British control.

DA: It was said that you write "with a sedate beauty that allows his character's emotions and inner lives to unfold with dignity and intelligence."

AC: The book did get a couple of praising reviews, including one very good one in *The Nation* by the film critic A.O. Scott. But I'm fully aware that the readership is mistrustful when a poet writes fiction. They think we don't really mean it. But actually I always loved fiction just as much as poetry. I wrote it early on but didn't get very far with it, I mean, in terms of publishing. Anyway, when someone seems dubious about my novelistic projects, I cite Thomas Hardy and go on about my business.

DA: Your second novel is set to come out later this year.

AC: It will appear in November with a new outfit in London called Eyewear Publishing. The title is *Miranda's Book*, and it is almost a historical novel, beginning in 1989 and continuing some time after that. The opening chapters are set in Cincinnati at the moment when the Contemporary Art Center there was prosecuted for mounting an exhibition of the photographs of Robert Mapplethorpe. One unusual character is a semi-retired novelist who belongs to a class that hasn't received much coverage in American fiction: that part of the African-American community that has been wealthy and upper crust for many generations. I did a lot of research about that group, to add to what I knew from having met a few of them.

DA: You certainly have a lot of teaching experience.

AC: In a lot of different places: the City University of New York, Columbia, the University of Cincinnati, Yale, Connecticut College, and UCLA. But this was nearly always an adjunct position. I was only a full-time professor for two years out of the twenty-odd I taught.

DA: What sort of courses did you teach—poetry workshops? Literature? French?

AC: As I said earlier I taught beginning French at Columbia for a couple of years, then abandoned that permanently. After my first book of poems appeared, I taught creative writing, poetry almost entirely. There was one course in short story, I think. And in the Graduate Writing Division at Columbia, apart from writing workshops, I was also allowed to teach courses in literature. Not regular graduate-style courses, with required articles or essays following MLA form, but instead the literary equivalent of "Physics for Poets." We looked at earlier literature with a view to plundering it for our own work. I also taught a course in prosody, you know, meter, rhyme, and verse form.

DA: Has teaching helped you as a writer and poet, staying connected with those trying to become writers?

AC: Yes it did, though I haven't taught for a decade now. It was my bizarre custom to stay in touch with students I regarded as promising, even after they were no longer students. And continue to offer assistance when I was asked for it. Many of them went on to publish, and probably a dozen or so now teach writing themselves. Two are Pulitzer Prize winners and another is a Chancellor of the Academy of American Poets. Several of them are magazine or book editors. And so on. In a few instances I've acted as a sort of mentor for people who never took any of my classes. Of course all this is time-consuming, but also rewarding in ways hard to describe.

DA: *Your book,* The Poem's Heartbeat: A Manual of Prosody, *was described by* Publishers' Weekly *as "A provocative, definitive manual."*

AC: It's my one "best-seller." I keep hoping that all its fans will turn to the books of poems themselves, but I won't be the first to remark that books about poetry find more readers than books of poetry. The book arose out of the prosody classes I taught at Columbia. I really had time over the years to hammer out ways of making the arcane subject of meter easier for the beginner to understand. Many people have told me that meter was Greek to them until they read this book. So I think it accomplished what it set out to do.

DA: *You also have written art criticism, as well as a book,* Aaron Rose: Photographs.

AC: Yes, I wrote an introduction to a collection of Rose's photographs and did an interview for the book, one just as detailed as what we're doing now.

DA: *What interested you so much about Aaron Rose?*

AC: I'd been writing reviews for *Art in America* and *ARTNews* for about ten years. Visual art is one of my enthusiasms, and we don't have so many skillful art critics just now. I was assigned to cover a show of Rose's photographs at a downtown gallery and wrote a praising review of it. When Abrams Books decided to publish a collection of his work, they asked him who should write the intro, and he put forward my name, even though we hadn't met. I was happy to do it because I truly and deeply admired his pictures. Many of them are cityscapes, and New York has always had a great fascination for me.

DA: It's nice you recognize the work of others, specifically, writing an introduction to Micah Towey's recent poetry collection, Whale of Desire.

AC: It's important for senior poets to call attention to the work of promising newcomers to the scene. Older poets did that for me. One day Micah will do that for poets younger than himself. That's how it works.

DA: You spend part of every year in the United Kingdom.

AC: My first long-term stay was in 1986, when I had a Guggenheim Fellowship. I repeated the experiment a year later. That's when I began writing my first novel, and it is, as I said, set in London. But I didn't return until late 1990s. There was another long-term stay in 2005, and since then I've spent a few months of every year either in London, or Cambridge, or in the North of England.

DA: I would guess you feel at home in London. You taught a course for the Poetry School there. And also one for the Arvon Foundation at Totleigh Barton, Devon.

AC: Yes, but mostly I'm there just to live—to see people, to attend theatre performances, see art exhibitions, and to write. My project at Clare Hall, Cambridge was to do a version of Rilke's *Duino Elegies*. It's not completed yet, but in the meantime Clare Hall made me a Life Fellow, so I can return if I decide to.

DA: Your play, Lowell's Bedlam, *opened in spring of 2011 at Pentameters Theatre in London.*

AC: Apart from poetry, I'd written a novel, short stories, literary criticism, autobiography, travel writing, and essays. So I thought why not a play? *Lowell's Bedlam* was the result. I met Robert Lowell on a couple of occasions and greatly admired him. Partly because he managed, despite chronic mental illness, to be a major poet. The public is interested in mental illness, and there have been plays about poets like Dickinson, Eliot, and Auden. Also, there was a film about Sylvia Plath and Ted Hughes. So Lowell's stay in a mental hospital struck me as a promising subject. It was well received in London, but I haven't found a place to stage it over here. That doesn't mean I've given up.

DA: I see you've entered the world of the electronic publishing. Your first ebook, Transatlantic Bridge: A Concise Guide to the Differences Between American and British English, *was published in 2012.*

AC: That's right. I took all of the notes I'd made over the years concerning the differences between British and American English and organized it into a book. The differences are many—not only vocabulary and pronunciation, but also grammar, spelling and punctuation. Also, the British have slang words we don't use. It's a book useful for the traveler, for readers over there and over here trying to understand works written in the alternative English (or films spoken in it), for actors, and for teachers of British or American literature. It addresses a problem no one seems to have focused on before. Of course we know that poetry in French has to be translated for an audience that doesn't know the language. But an obstacle for British books being read here is that translations aren't provided. Also, in poetry sound has an overriding importance. If you don't know how the poem sounded to the author, have you fully understood the poem? I don't think so.

DA: Guess, poetry and writing, have come a long way since our college days, who would have imagined?

AC: They have, but I think it's still recognizable. It must be poetry because what else on earth could it possibly be?

Published in *Pif Magazine* April 1st, 2014

Poetry by Alfred Corn

The Unknown Poets

1.

Who, glimpsing her crow silhouette
Against a lamplit wall that night
Of fog and mizzle, would ever know?
A damp trudge home with headcold sniffles,
which had been maddening to stifle
during the long hour while a famous
name recited to a packed house.

The mirror gives her a strange look
So she reopens his new book
and tries to read. It's useless, though.
You'd almost prefer something uncouth.
If asked, she'd turn from the bookshelves
to say, We write of course for ourselves—
and no doubt blush for the half-truth.

2.
The laureate he most admired wrote
back, just once. A world of finesse
in small black script! The other letters
went unanswered, which hurt, but then
it freed him from at least the guilt
that goes with stealing time from writers
who need their hours at the desk.

Bless Dickinson! He told a friend
the story of her handmade booklets.
His own best efforts cried and pled,
So at last he had them printed and bound
At the copier's: one blue, one red,

one black. Felice, after he died,
would read them, once. And when she died…

3.
Original but quiet, you didn't
know a soul, no one who read much.
Sometimes perception stood and spoke,
And the ground buckled, planets wheeled—.
But feeling *alone*'s no guarantee.
What to do with all these unsent
messages, put them in a bottle?
Plenty of empties lay around.
A page took down the pangs, line
upon line. And then? Then turned. Was gone.
At dusk, high treetops strained against
word and structure, each backlit leaf
rattling, shooting the dark rapids…
And day dawned with a perfect stillness.

Robert Dana

Robert Dana (1929-2010), Poet Laureate for the state of Iowa at the time of this interview, has published 10 collections of poetry, including his most recent *The Morning of the Red Admirals* (Anhinga Press, 2004). His previous poetry collections include *Starting Out for the Difficult World* (Harper & Row, 1987), which was short listed for the 1998 Pulitzer Prize; *Yes, Everything* (Another Chicago Press, 1994); *Hello, Stranger: Beach Poems* (Anhinga Press, 1996); and *Summer* (Anhinga Press, 2000).

Dana also was the editor of *Against the Grain: Interviews with Maverick American Publishers* (University of Iowa Press, 1986) and *A Community of Writers: Paul Engle and the Iowa Writers' Workshop* (University of Iowa Press, 1999).

Photo © Anhinga Press

Born in Boston, Dana moved to Iowa and graduated from Drake University and the Iowa Writers' Workshop. He taught for 40 years at Cornell College, where he was Poet-in-Residence. He has also served as Distinguished Visiting Writer at Stockholm University and at several American colleges and universities.

His poetry has been widely hailed, winning several awards, including two National Endowment of the Arts Fellowships, The Delmore Schwartz Memorial Award from New York University in 1989, and the 1994 Carl Sandburg Medal for Poetry.

Dana was honored earlier this year at the annual AWP (American Writers and Writing Programs) Conference in Atlanta by a panel, chaired by novelist and poet R.M. Ryan, entitled "A Celebration of Robert Dana," consisting of fellow poets and writers David Lynn of *The Kenyon Review*, Stephen Corey of *The Georgia Review*, David Hamilton of *The Iowa Review*, and Hilda Raz of *Prairie Schooner*.

Derek Alger: That was quite a tribute to you at the most recent AWP Conference, a sort of coming together of poets past, present and future.

Robert Dana: Yes, it was a humbling experience. I was spooked by the idea when it was first brought to my attention. But I was also honored to think that so many of my younger colleagues wanted to do this. And it certainly did bring together many writers and editors from across nearly 40 or 50 years of my literary life. They make up a kind of extended literary family, I suppose.

DA: Sometimes others see us better than ourselves.

RD: I was certainly reminded of many things I'd forgotten. And so many people to think I'd done work that was worthy of this kind of notice.

DA: It's probably fair to say that your childhood was not conventional.

RD: I was orphaned at the age of eight in Boston when my mother died and my father deserted my half sister and I. Being put in foster homes certainly alters one's perspective. Without family, you're at the bottom of the social and economic scale. I guess I still tend to look at things from the bottom up.

DA: Do you remember writing or having a gift for language during your younger more turbulent years?

RD: Well, I was a terrific liar, a fabulist, I suppose you might say, if you wanted to put a kinder spin on it. In grade school, I made up stories about my father, saying that he owned a horse farm in Virginia and that I had a horse there. I suppose I was trying to create status for myself.
    On the more serious side, I also had to try to make sense of the incomprehensible thing that had happened to me. I spent a lot of time in walking the railroad tracks at night, talking to the sky, asking God why this terrible thing was happening to me. Of course, he never answered. I also spent a lot of time alone in the woods. The small town where I

grew up was at the bottom of the Berkshires. So I became something of a naturalist. I probably knew more about birds, snakes, and trees than I did about classmates.

The town also had a tiny library which doubled as a social center on Friday nights. In addition to a multi-volume Natural History which I became addicted to, I also encountered there the poetry of Wordsworth, Coleridge, Keats, Shelley. Grimm's Fairy Tales. And the poetry of Edgar Allan Poe. Wordsworth connected to my interest in Nature and Poe's darkness seemed to match my own. Of course, I never encountered the work of any modern writers until I entered college.

DA: Serving in the Navy must have given you a wider perspective of the world.

RD: It certainly did. I served on Guam in the South Pacific for a year and a half. The war was officially over by then, but there were armed Japanese soldiers still holed up in the Southern half of the island. Many of my Navy pals were older and more experienced men. One or two even had university degrees.

When I returned to the states in `48, I enrolled at Holyoke Jr. College in Holyoke, Massachusetts. It was the first of what are now called Community Colleges. In those days, it borrowed its faculty from Smith, Mt. Holyoke, and other blue ribbon schools. And once I started to read and become aware of the richness of the world, I was a student on fire.

My best friend back then was my roommate Joe Kohler. He'd been a bombardier on B-24's making runs through German flak over Romanian oil fields. He was 26. A soft-spoken guy from Baltimore with a sly sense of humor. We roomed in the attic space of an old mansion that was being used as a temporary YMCA. We were so poor back then that we'd often share a pack of cigarettes, stubbing the last one of the night only half smoked to save for the next morning.

DA: Then it was on to college at Drake University.

RD: Yes, when I arrived at Drake I'd already abandoned several versions of myself (jazz musician, philosopher) and decided to be a journalist and novelist a la Hemingway. And I actually worked as a newspaper reporter in Des Moines both of my undergraduate years there.

DA: But you discovered you were a poet.

RD: Another one of those fortunate accidents of my life. I was assigned as an advisee to E.L. Mayo who, I would learn later, was a major American poet. Ed, who was also from Boston, took an interest in my writing.

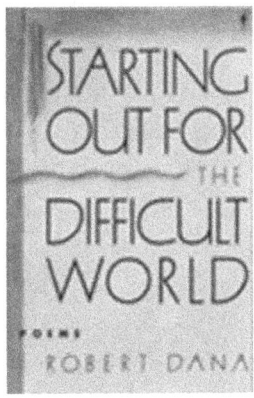

At that time, I had trouble finishing short stories. Ed pointed out to me that I was trying to make every word perfect, so I'd start revising the piece before I got three pages into it. He pointed out that this way of writing was more common among poets than prose writers. He then asked if I'd ever written poetry. I had, of course written the kind of bad poems many of us wrote to girls we had a crush on, the kind that convinced them that they were right: we were weird. I didn't subject him to any of the silliness I'd written up until then.

I did take his Modern Poetry course where I finally encountered all the wonderful poets whose work I loved and was moved by, and whose poems would become so important to me the rest of my life. I began to write poetry seriously then, and I've never looked back.

DA: You edited a book on Paul Engle and the Iowa Writers' Workshop where you quote Engle as saying the workshop was there to offer young, aspiring writers "hard criticism and decent sympathy."

RD: The workshop was in its infancy then, of course. My class with John Berryman, for example, had only thirteen people in it. But I think Paul's statement describes perfectly what the workshop was all about back then.

DA: Did you find the workshop at Iowa similar to a sidewalk cafe in Paris in an earlier day?

RD: Well, I don't really know much about what actually happened between writers at Paris cafés. I think Workshop is a term that really describes what went on at Iowa in the 1950's. It was something more akin to a bunch of very knowledgeable guys in a local garage arguing over how best to build this hot car. What kind of streamlining should the fenders have? Do we even need fenders? How much horsepower does it need? What about overhead cams? And for Christ's sake get rid of that hood ornament!

DA: You had an unusual commute to the Iowa Writers Workshop.

RD: Yes, I hitchhiked twenty-six miles to the university every day, winter and summer. I was taking a full schedule of graduate classes and I don't recall ever missing a class.

DA: You were fortunate to be with quite a group of poets in the workshops taught by Robert Lowell and John Berryman.

RD: The Berryman class, in particular, was remarkable. Many of its members already had graduate degrees from other schools—Harvard, North Carolina, and so on—in some cases, two degrees. They were exceptionally well read. They understood poetic form. And they wrote well. I was the youngest member of the class, a marginal man, so to speak, and not as well prepared as I would like to have been.

Before we left Iowa, several members of the class—Donald Justice and Henri Coulette among them—had already begun to publish in major American magazines.

DA: When you were at Iowa, the emphasis really wasn't on establishing a literary career.

RD: I don't recall anyone talking as if they expected to make a living writing poetry. Our hopes were more modest: to teach English or American literature somewhere and to write well.

Jobs were terribly scarce in the mid-1950's. There were, with the exception of Stanford, no other writing programs out there. Teaching what is now called Creative Writing wasn't an option. And many of the academic teaching jobs had already been snapped up by the preceding generation of GI Bill people with graduate degrees.

Justice wound up at Hamline, Coulette at a high school in a tough part of L.A., Philip Levine at Fresno State College—and everybody, however restless, felt lucky to be employed.

DA: Obviously you found a home teaching at Cornell College.

RD: Another lucky break. After 150 letters of application went glimmering, I phoned Tom Dunn who was the head of the Drake English Department. He knew of the Cornell opening and set up an interview for me. It turned out they wanted someone to take over a bunch of journalism courses and advise the student newspaper and the yearbook staff. On the side, I'd teach a couple of sophomore literature courses.

Over the years, I began publishing poetry in *Poetry*, *The Paris Review*, and other important magazines, and I was gradually able to move into teaching literature full time.

DA: You had an interesting opportunity to talk one on one with Robert Frost.

RD: Yes, I was spending the summer on an old farmstead in Rochester, Vermont, across the White River from Ripton. My first wife and my two daughters were with me. I paid him a visit one afternoon, and it turned into a once a week talk session for three weeks. He was generous with his time, helpful, intelligent, and contrary to his folksy public image, thoroughly read. Not only did he know his Bible and Greek Drama and mythology, he could quote you the best poem or two from books by good but minor poets among his contemporaries,

I had yet to write a successful poem of any kind. I wrote perhaps two or three flawed pieces a year. When I complained to Frost about this, he asked me, "Have you read my *Collected Poems*? How many poems do you think that amounts to in a year?" I made a quick calculation and said, "About ten or 12." "Yes," he said, and some of those I throw away. Be patient. Keep working. It will come," he assured me. And I felt as if a great weight had been lifted from my shoulders. A year or two later, I broke through.

Published in *Pif Magazine* July 26th, 2007

Poetry by Robert Dana

RAPTURE

In the thick, Carolina night,
the great luggage of the sea
falls thudding and trundling
and tumbling up the stairs of
beach; its undertow hissing,
sometimes spitting, rolling
back on its own prolonged
susurrations; pouring in
loud hushes across planking
through the open bedroom door;
flooding room and mirror;
overwhelming our breathing;
drowning, almost, even sleep
in which something deeper
hurries away, and the day
repeats and repeats itself
like the heaven of the waves,
and we waken again to thrum
of diesel and the raging sun.

Ani Gjika

Ani Gjika was born and raised in Albania, before moving to the United States with her parents at the age of 18 and studying poetry at Simmons College and Boston University. Her poetry collection, *Bread on Running Waters*, published by Fenway Press (http://www.fenwaypress.com), was a finalist for the 2011 Anthony Hecht Poetry Prize, 2011 May Sarton New Hampshire Book Prize and 2011 Crab Orchard Series Award. She is a 2010 Robert Pinsky Global Fellow and winner of a 2010 Robert Fitzgerald Translation Prize. Poems and translations have appeared or are forthcoming in *Ploughshares, AGNI Online, Salamander, Seneca Review, World Literature Today, Two Lines Online, From the Fishouse* and elsewhere.

Derek Alger: I find it amazing English is your second language, especially after reading your poetry.

Ani Gjika: Thank you, Derek. But I honestly feel that I live in the realm of the semi-inarticulate. I left my home country of Albania when I was 18 to move to the United States. I studied some English when I was eight years old back in Albania, but didn't really learn to speak the language until after moving here and taking up an English major in the late '90s. Since then, English has become my first language and yet, I am aware of how limited my English lexicon is. And the same is true of my Albanian lexicon. I feel like I have one foot in each language, far apart from each other, and therefore never able to stand up straight.

DA: Your parents were a strong influence on you.

AG: They were and still are. If it weren't for them, I would have probably never gotten into languages so early in my life. They arranged for me to study English and Italian with a private tutor and then later, major in Russian in high school. Very few people took Russian in high school back then. English and German were the popular foreign languages. And even though I felt like my parents were dictating this choice for me, I immediately loved Russian and I had the sense that if I didn't, they would have allowed me the option to switch to something else.

We lived in a 650 sq. ft. apartment for the first 18 years of my life, but we owned a decent number of books. My earliest memories are of my parents being at work, my grandmother sitting on her bed reading her Bible and me sitting on the floor in the living room browsing through these heavy, chocolate colored, hard-cover Encyclopedias of Russian Literature. The books were filled with lots of what seemed to me magical, black and white illustrations. Thank god for Google, here's a picture of one of them: http://minsk.mn.slando.by/obyavlenie/kratkaya-literaturnaya-entsiklopediya-kle-ID4ehtl.html

There were also smaller books two of which I remember vividly because they had a soft green cover, the text inside was arranged differently, and they were written by strangely named authors or had strange titles like Gitanjali (years later I made the connection to Tagore) and Walt Whitman (the "w" is not a letter in the Albanian alphabet). There was also my mother's own first book of poetry on the cover of which I drew circles because I knew it was hers and in my head I think I was simply claiming it, not destroying it. My father, who was a professor of Albanian linguistics and did a lot of research and writing in the city's main library, would often bring home books from there. Albanian and Greek myths and legends were my favorites. I remember I couldn't wait to finish reading Aeschylus so I could start over again.

DA: What was your early schooling like?

AG: It felt pretty regimented. I remember having to show up early and line up in the courtyard, go through the physical exercise routine, then sing some sort of hymn to the Communist Party or Enver Hoxha and finally go inside to my classes. The whole uniformity of it all used to make me very nervous. We had to follow strict moves, sing specific songs at a specific pitch, wear uniforms. But it was also a simpler time that seems like forever ago. I lived in the capital city and went to good schools, but there was no central heating in our classrooms. Sometimes the glass was broken on the windows and replaced with plastic wrap. We had a very small wood stove in the center of each classroom and that was supposed to heat the entire room. Everyone kept their jackets on in the winter. And at lunch time, I loved toasting bread on top of that stove taking turns with my classmates. Sometimes our teacher wouldn't go to the teachers' office, but stay back and have plain toast and butter with us. Really, sounds like such an innocent world from centuries ago. I haven't even thought of this until now. Geez.

Around the end of my first grade, in April 1985, Enver Hoxha, who had been Albania's Communist leader since 1944, died. I remember vividly how some teachers gathered a couple of the classes and took us all on a walk to a field nearby. And there they told us. But they were crying and shaking and then my classmates started crying and I felt really weird, like they were joking or acting or something. I remember trying to cry too but nothing was coming. I think I probably finally did, after a while. But then remember going home and finding my grandmother also crying and so I sat down and wrote my first poem and it was all about April and tears and it all rhymed. I was kind of thrilled.

DA: A stroke of luck changed your life.

AG: Definitely did. When I was 17, my father came home one day clapping and dancing, saying that he'd won the lottery. He was talking about the U.S. Diversity Immigrant Visa he had just won and him being head of household meant that my mother, my brother and I had, too. The U.S. offers this visa annually to residents of countries that have lower immigrant rates in the States. A year later, after all the paperwork had been filed, we flew to Massachusetts. My parents didn't speak any English when we got here. They were highly educated people who suddenly had to make a living as dishwashers and custodians here and yet they kept doing what they love and know how to do well. My mother has continued to write poetry and my father continues to write critical essays and books on Albanian historical and literary figures.

DA: Your early English lessons paid off.

AG: Well, to some extent. I mean, sure, I was the translator in my family for a while and I had definitely learned the basics of grammar. But I remember struggling my first years in college. I would read the materials, understand individual words but have no clue about the meaning of entire paragraphs. I took ESL classes for a semester. Then regular classes as a business major, kind of following what my parents said was a smart career choice. Then I took advanced comp. and literature electives and knew right away that this was what I wanted to study, forever. I talked it over with my parents and they got convinced. So I switched majors my sophomore year. Becoming an English major is what eventually made me fluent in English. At Atlantic Union College, where I completed my undergraduate studies, I was introduced to Emily Dickinson, Robert Frost, the Transcendentalists, Wallace Stevens, W.B. Yeats. I worked in the school's library and was in charge of maintaining "The Special Collection Room" which carried numerous works by the best 20th century American poets. I would go in there to dust or add books on the shelves and sometimes couldn't resist stopping to read a page from Elizabeth Bishop's letters, or a poem by A. R. Ammons or Louis MacNeice, or to just look, one more time, at a Rupert Brooke photo. I don't know how to explain that room's significance to my introduction to American poetry or how it influenced how I started to look at language. I haven't thought of it in years. Now that I think about it, I never really went after books or poetry. They happened to be available wherever I was. I realize now, because of this conversation with you, how extremely fortunate I've been knowing how impossible it was for my parents' generation to have access to literature, or anything really, in such an abundant and relaxed way.

DA: And then you went to Simmons College.

AG: This is really weird. Now that I'm thinking back to all these stages I've been through the years, I'm realizing how each one has been profoundly meaningful and crucial to where I am today and why I've been able to finally complete this first book of poems. While working on my MA in English at Simmons, I fell in love with the postmodernists (Kundera in particular) and James Joyce and rediscovered Yeats again in David Gullette's classes. Here, it was David who took an interest in my poetry and although we didn't have a creative writing class together, he was the first teacher I had to give me feedback on a manuscript as a whole. He could call out bullshit right away and made me aware of what a difference a line break makes. From 2000-2004, I had also been a regular participant in online poetry workshops which were very useful to me. One of those forums in particular, what was then called "the sandbox," is where I met poets that I'm still in touch with today. That forum has been as important and as meaningful to me as "The Special Collection Room" was at AUC.

DA: You then found yourself in an unexpected place.

AG: I went to teach in Thailand right after Simmons. It was the perfect first teaching job. I worked in both the English and ESL departments at Asia Pacific International University, a Christian school. I taught literature, creative writing and language classes. My students were from all over Southeast Asia, a few from Europe and the Middle East. I lived and worked there for four years. I visited India frequently because my ex-husband is from there. The weather in those countries was overwhelming at times, but it was coupled with the beautiful sounds of geckos and koyals (nightingales) and unbelievably long periods of rain. I didn't understand this new language, but there were stray dogs everywhere, tuk-tuk drivers, beggars, coolies (the people who'll carry your luggage at train stations in India), family owned side-of-the-road restaurants and I didn't need a language to move in and out of these spaces they belonged to. Being in these new landscapes I felt a strong sense that I'd find home anywhere I went and that at the same time, none of these places were for me to own.

DA: Then on to Boston University.

AG: In 2009, I decided I wanted to do an MFA. I only applied to Boston University and, luckily, got in. My experience at BU has humbled me. The program is really small (in my year, there were only 8 poets) and everyone has a unique style and voice. For the first time in my life I was workshopping poems in a group of highly talented people. I felt ambitious at first, then pretty ordinary, then realized that the strengths everyone had were a testament to the high expectations and strengths of the program. I learned a little later into the program that being there with those other 7 poets and our incredibly talented faculty (Robert Pinsky, Louise Glück and Rosanna Warren in poetry), it was never about whose work was better than whose, but about what each of us could learn from one another. Robert often inspired me to really understand this. BU provided, for me, a very comfortable place where I truly thrived in the company of really talented people and where I could finally come back to and focus on my manuscript.

DA: In her introduction to Bread on Running Waters, *Rosanna Warren, states, you have turned your adopted language of English "into a subtle instrument, a beautifully judged voicing that never slides into self-pity or melodrama."*

AG: I am deeply honored that Rosanna wrote that introduction. I have read that line many times. I have read it, but I wish I could own it the way you own something you know. English, for me, is a constant reminder of how inadequate I am in public. I never feel comfortable using it unless it's just me and the page. I sometimes think that I chose to write in this language because this language allows me to be honest and frank in a way that I couldn't trust Albanian to allow me. For the longest time growing up, Albanian was the language of politicians, harassers, secrets, prejudice, persecutions and people who lied and corrupted left and right. I think I must have subconsciously rejected it when I discovered those 20th century poets whose language spoke to a side of me that constantly felt ambushed on back in Albania.

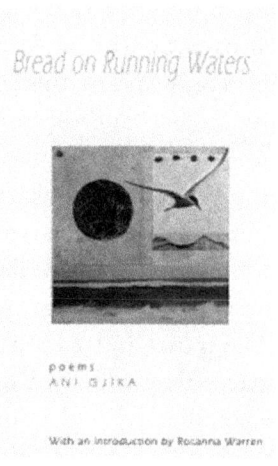

DA: It's fitting the first section of your poetry collection is titled "Goodbye Enver Hoxha."

AG: Yes, thank you for bringing that up. Titling that first section "Goodbye Enver Hoxha" was my way of giving Hoxha and everything he represented to my childhood imagination the same kind of treatment

I would give a toy I'd grown weary of. Enver Hoxha, for those first 6-7 years of my life was a kind of toy, a puppet if you will. He was always on TV. Everyone clapped and sang for him. His name was written in big red letters everywhere I looked. Don't get me wrong, everyone lived under extreme stress and anxiety for many years before and after he died. You only have to think of what the Soviet Union was like under Stalin, to the power of two, to have an idea what it was like in Albania. That kind of anxiety metastasizes and is hereditary through generations I think. But I and all the kids in that first section of my book were children when he died. And childhood is untouched by tyranny and oppression. A child doesn't understand the death penalty, political prisoners, evictions of families, people controlled by the secret police. I wanted to convey that while he spread terror over the whole land for half a century, that's all he was to the children—a strange toy we have, unanimously, said goodbye to before any of the adults could.

DA: Tell us a bit about how the long poem "In Her Father's House" came about?

AG: I wanted to create something of the feel of theater, get the reader to experience a poem like a play. We had been reading *King Lear* in one of Rosanna Warren's classes at BU. So I started out by setting up the stage with those berry bushes whispering. I was interested in exploring another complex father-daughter story. I had lost my aunt in 2008. The circumstances around the death of the father in this poem closely reflect the strange circumstances of her death. I just switched the genders of the protagonists and the rest is my best attempt at blurring the lines between genres of writing. I had planned to have all these characters and voices, but it's mainly a one-woman play.

DA: And today you're a teacher.

AG: I've been teaching since 2003 and can't imagine something more satisfying or a better place to grow. I teach advanced language and composition classes at Massachusetts International Academy to Chinese high school and college graduates who plan to pursue a higher education in the U.S.

DA: What comes next?

AG: Writing much better poems I hope. Read more widely. Challenge myself. My mother writes in Albanian. I've been translating some of her poetry and other Albanian poets off and on. I'd like to make something concrete out of that in a couple of years.

Published in *Pif Magazine* April 1st, 2013

Poems by Ani Gjika

PORTRAIT OF A COUPLE ON THE GRASS
on a photograph of George and Mary Oppen

They have survived one another.
The earth holds them the way it holds
children: gladly and curiously affected.

His silver head piles its years on her lap.
His body seems borrowed, already an absence.
Her right hand maps his temples, his forehead.

What does the grass ask for, and the Japanese
knotweed behind them? His hand inside his pocket,
what is it holding, or her eyes under those glasses?

Here, he will sleep forever
and the shadows of trees will never
stretch long enough to enter their bodies.

Here, everything is an instant of tension –
shapes continuously touching, perching
so that one's weight never cancels the other's.

WHITE NOISE

We sat around our small table,
the balcony French doors wide open
to the breeze, the flies.
I could hear the neighbors above
and my friend Miri, chasing a tire down the street.

Each family eavesdropped on the next like clockwork.

My mother ladled soup in four bowls.
I remember her white ankles
taking her
in and out of the kitchen
and my father
never moving to help her.
He liked to watch her
like I did.

We sat together like this only on Sundays.
Grandmother translated for us from Greek:
"throw your bread on running waters
and you'll see that it comes back to you".
She'd hide the book under her pillow,
then finally sit down to eat.

Nobody I loved was taken into the woods and shot.

In the summer, I met my half-brother
for the first time, his head shaved like a soldier's.
He came back to us when I didn't know
how to know him. At supper, my father
didn't know how to help either:
he made jokes about girls
then asked about his grades.

When my parents visit us,
I prepare a meal, pass the bread, wait for a toast

and sit quietly, like my father, listening
to everyone's insignificant confessions.
We hardly ever talk of his son
who lives permanently away.
Somehow all absence of speech
replaces his absence,
or everyone's regrets,
or everything that's been thrown away.

At the landing, they turn to wave goodbye
looking up at us.
My father's silver head looks smaller
every time I see him.
The parenthesis around my mother's mouth
more prominent now
from withholding.

My husband shuts the door.
It's windy out. I part the curtains
and watch them get in the car, watch
whatever is rushing against them.

Kelle Groom

Kelle Groom (http://www.kellegroom.com) is the author of the memoir, *I Wore the Ocean in the Shape of a Girl* (Free Press/Simon & Schuster 2011), which was a Barnes & Noble Discover Great Writers pick, as well as a *New York Times Book Review* Editor's Choice selection, a *Library Journal* Best Memoir of 2011, a Barnes & Noble Book of the Month, an *Oxford American* Editor's Pick, and Oprah.com *O Magazine* selection. "In stirring, hypnotic prose," Groom's memoir tells of her struggle with addiction, and the loss of her son, first to adoption when she was nineteen, and then, after being diagnosed with leukemia, to his death at the age of only fourteen months.

Groom is also the author of three poetry collections, *Five Kingdoms* (Anhinga Press, 2010), *Luckily* (Anhinga Press, 2006), and *Underwater City* (University Press of Florida 2004). Her poetry has appeared in *Best American Poetry 2010*, *The New Yorker*, *Ploughshares*, and *Poetry*, among many other literary journals and publications. She has received special mention in the *Pushcart Prize 2010* and *Best American Non-Required Reading 2007* anthologies.

Groom is the recipient of fellowships from Black Mountain Institute, Millay Colony for the Arts, Atlantic Center for the Arts, and Virginia Center for the Creative Arts, to name a few, as well as both a 2010 and a 2006 Florida Book Award. She is Distinguished Writer-in-Residence (2012-2013) in the Sierra Nevada College English Department, and is also on the faculty of the low-residency MFA program at Sierra Nevada College, Lake Tahoe. A former poetry editor of *The Florida Review*, she is now a contributing editor.

Derek Alger: One source of continuity in your life is clear from your statement about how you "Always went back to the Cape."

Kelle Groom: I've spent a lot of my life moving. Over fifty different places, half of those before I was twenty years old. Both of my parents are from Massachusetts, my mom's family from Cape Cod. My grandparents lived in South Yarmouth and Dennis all their lives. A few years after my Dad joined the Navy, we left the Cape, but we came home every summer. I still try to return every year.

DA: Another example of continuity in your life was, of course, writing.

KG: I recall learning to read and beginning to write poems and stories as happening at the same time. I loved the way another world opens up in both. It seemed as if the only way to understand something was to write about it. I always wrote—as a kid, in my teens, into adulthood, drunk, sober.

DA: You certainly moved around with your family.

KG: Yes, I spent my early childhood in Massachusetts. But even there, we moved several times. I was born in Brockton, but never lived in that city. We were living in Whitman, but my mother didn't want to give birth in a military hospital. A year later, we spent the winter in a summer rental on Bass River, among other places. My grandfather was a builder, and he built our last home on the mid-Cape, in Dennisport. We left it for Hawaii—Waipahu and Honolulu, then Orlando, El Paso, Satellite Beach in Florida, the coast of Spain near Cadiz. I graduated from high school there. I'd published my first story at fifteen, in my school's literary magazine.

DA: College was rather a rude awakening at first, though, I must admit I had a similar experience.

KG: I'd graduated from high school a year early, and my parents would only allow me to attend my mother's school, Bridgewater State College in Massachusetts. They were still stationed overseas, and wanted me to have family nearby. On my college application, I'd written that I wanted to be a writer. I'd done well in English. But in my first literature class, we analyzed poems, and I was told my answers were wrong. It was disorienting, as if literature had become math. I made a C. I'd never made a C in anything but algebra. It reminded me of my college music class. My teacher would play music, and then ask us to write about it. I had no idea what he meant, so I wrote images and scenes. Made a D in music.

My first semester, I was on academic probation. I started drinking before my 8 a.m. class. But it was a class I audited that saved me. The class certified me to work a Suicide Hotline off-campus. I'd had self-destructive thoughts and hoped the class could give me some tips on staying alive. I did get certified, and was also befriended by an older classmate who connected me to a community and support. I'd found out about the class at a family party in Brockton. A woman mysteriously related to me, who I never saw before or since, told me about this class. All around me were my dad's relatives, most of whom I'd never met. I kept hearing strangers say, "That's Mike's girl."

DA: Then you found an academic home at the University of Central Florida.

KG: Yes. I received my BA, MA, and MFA from UCF. When I left Bridgewater, I went to a community college in Florida. I almost flunked out, and went to see an academic counselor. She said that since I made As in my Creative Writing classes, I should only take Creative Writing. I think I took four sections of it, and my grade point average stabilized. I was pregnant at the time, and following the pregnancy, drinking alcoholically. But I went on to UCF for my BA, and though I dropped out several times, one of my first writing teachers, Wyatt Wyatt continued to visit me at work and encourage me to return to school. Wyatt always made me feel as if I were not only okay, but interesting. If it had felt like pity, as if he were doing me a favor, it wouldn't have worked. But I felt that Wyatt genuinely missed me and valued my writing. He introduced me to other writers. Wyatt invited me to a dinner with Harry Crews, and it meant so much to me to sit at that table when I was twenty years old and not yet sober.

Don Stap was also a great supporter at UCF. He created the student literary magazine, *The Cypress Dome,* in which I published my first poem and won first place in their literary contest. He continued to support me throughout my academic career, and I received awards for outstanding undergraduate poet and graduate student. I'd never had the word "outstanding" applied to anything I'd done before. When I returned to UCF for my MFA, Don was my thesis advisor. He nominated my thesis for the University's Thesis Award—one thesis chosen from every thesis in every college that year. It won.

DA: You originally were writing prose but decided to concentrate on poetry.

KG: I wrote both, but in graduate school, we had to choose a concentration. I love the distillation of poetry, the direct line to feeling and emotion. I continued to write prose, including flash fiction, in my graduate workshops, but focused primarily on poetry in school.

DA: You experienced the stress and scramble of adjunct teaching after college.

KG: While working on my MA in Creative Writing, I'd been teaching English as a Second Language full-time. But when the private language school hired a new director, faculty were required to have an MA in Linguistics. I was out of a job and mentioned this in passing to Wyatt Wyatt, who was still teaching at UCF then. He'd immediately marched me down the hall to the Chair of English Department and announced, "Kelle is available to teach!" As if it were the luckiest thing in the world. I was very lucky to have had Wyatt as a champion. I did teach seven classes at four different campuses that semester, and ran a car into the ground. But the next semester, UCF gave me five sections of composition to teach. It was valuable teaching experience, and it helped me in a tough time. But I couldn't live on it and had no insurance. For another semester, I managed a bookstore full-time and taught two classes. At the same time, I ran a non-profit literary arts organization, liquid poetry, that I'd created as a graduate student. I'd learned to do grassroots fundraising for liquid poetry, and loved the work. I found the persuasive skills I'd learned in teaching argument in composition lent themselves to grant writing. It led me to other nonprofit organizations, and I spent the next decade working for them.

DA: The acclaimed poet and writer, Kelly Cherry, was an inspiration for you.

KG: When I was an undergraduate, Kelly Cherry visited UCF. She read from her memoir, *The Exiled Heart*. After she'd left, Wyatt told me that he'd spoken to Kelly about my writing. Kelly said, "Tell her to write me a letter." I was thrilled, but couldn't imagine how to do it. It was several years later that I wrote a poem, "Letter to Kelly Cherry." I mailed it to her. I also invited Kelly to read in the liquid poetry series. Luckily, she was able to return to Orlando for an unforgettable reading. Andy Solomon, who was the English Department Chair at University of Tampa, drove down to interview her for our author video series. It was such a joy to hear Kelly read again and to talk with her.

In *The Exiled Heart*, Kelly had left everything behind in a little room in Amsterdam. My poem, "Letter to Kelly Cherry," asks her how to leave everything, to take a train into the wilderness. I recall that as she traveled by train into the Soviet Union, each station was progressively grayer, more drab. But her departure from everything known thrilled me. I lived in a museum of my life. A stranger coming into my apartment said, "It's like walking into a poem." Every space was covered with bookshelves, books, poems tacked to the walls and taped to mirrors, posters for book covers, photographs. My life felt so heavy, and I didn't know how to move anymore. I kept thinking about *The Exiled Heart*. The beautiful music of Kelly's poems stays with me too. One of my favorites is "Gethsemane" which I've loved since first reading it in the *Atlantic* in 1988.

DA: Your first collection of poetry, Underwater City, *explores borders separating individuals, with powerful poems ranging from a Civil War battlefield to a laundry room.*

KG: In *Underwater City*, there are a number of elegiac poems, for my grandmother and for my son. I wrote the poems I needed. When I didn't know what to do with grief, I turned to form. After my grandmother died, I took her Methodist Hymnal. In it, I found "The Order for the Burial of a Child." I hadn't been present at my son's burial, and it took me seventeen years to find his grave. I needed some kind of form to begin to write about this, so I took "The Order" from the Hymnal. In writing about my grandmother's death, I began with a pantoum and changed it slightly. I was unable to let go of her, and the pantoum was perfect as it allowed us to simply stay in one moment. I also began writing poems that used ekphrastic elements. "Pinhole Camera" began with Marian Roth's photographs. Marian was incredibly kind to me and allowed me to select one of her stunning images for the cover of the book. I began writing about violence as well, with "Drowning, 1983," using an image of an abandoned lighthouse to get at what had been done to a woman's body. There are also love poems in this first collection. In some, as in "The Boy with His Mother Inside Him," love and grief together. Judith Hemschemyer was the series editor for the Contemporary Poetry Series at University Press of Florida, and I was very happy when she selected *Underwater City*. The series had existed for twenty years, and mine was the last collection published.

DA: Your next two collections, Luckily *and* Five Kingdoms, *demonstrate you as a poet who has mastered a wide range of emotion, with intelligence, passion, and above all, fierce honesty.*

KG: If at the ground of the poem, I'm not being honest, it's doomed from the start. It's just rococo or ego, some kind of decoration. It has to start out of my own confusion and/or need for the poem. In *Luckily*, I experimented more with tone, and I also continued to write about violence toward women. Rick Campbell and Lynne Knight run Anhinga Press. They selected *Luckily* for their Florida Poetry Series. Rick and Lynne are incredibly generous advocates for poetry. I am forever grateful for their limitless support, love of poetry, and friendship. In *Five Kingdoms*, also published by Anhinga, I was interested in the idea of safety and what safety means. The title poem was written on the 60th anniversary of the atomic bombing of Hiroshima. It's non-narrative, composed of a series of questions regarding personal and national security. I used a language of fear and superstition to question what we're willing to sacrifice to be safe. The first section explores political themes and addresses subjects across a broad expanse of time—the oldest bones of the first human child found in Ethiopia, the oldest map of the world found near Baghdad, the bombing of Fallujah. I was interested in the connection between physical and metaphysical worlds. Voices of the dead and the living. In the second section, the focus narrows from the world to the city. The theme of shelter is important. The third section of *Five Kingdoms* narrows to the individual. The predominant tone is elegiac. Political themes recur, as do ekphrastic elements, in the examination of individual lives and the search for physical and metaphysical shelter.

DA: Your earlier poetry seems like a warmup to get to the point where you could write your memoir, I Wore the Ocean in the Shape of a Girl.

KG: No, not at all. I don't think of poetry as a warm-up to anything. I did first write about grief and violence and loss in my poems. Though I wrote about these in prose as well. I also kept journals documenting these events, trying to make sense of them. I am primarily a poet. Any prose I write is indebted to my training as a poet. I want both poems and prose that say what can't be said. In writing my memoir, I had a task. I hoped that by writing about my son, it would take me to him. I also hoped to find the girl I'd been—to see what had happened to her and to speak for her.

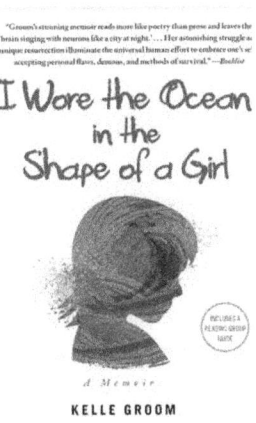

DA: Many others have been inspired by how you survived the unimaginable.

KG: I don't think what happened to me is unimaginable. One woman who wrote to me, said, "No one talks about these things." Then she told me her story. Each person who wrote to me connected with some part of the book. It's about loss, but it's also about survival and love and wanting to live. Another person wrote to tell me about her mother who as a young girl in Ireland had been forced to give up her child. She said that her mother has dementia now, and all she talks about is the child she gave away. Someone else wrote to tell me about her struggles with addiction. She said she'd never written to an author before, that she didn't need a response. "I just wanted you to know I'm okay," she said. People have pulled me aside at readings to tell me what happened to them. Just wanting to tell me, to say it. Because I had said it, I was someone who could listen. Nick Flynn told me that my memoir would have its own life. People have their own experience with the book. I'm grateful when they tell me about it.

DA: The range of conflicting emotions at the time must have been confusing and intense.

KG: I'm not sure what you mean. Do you mean during my life in my teens and early 20s? Yes, of course, but I always wrote. The writing felt like it was saving me. And then, when I was on that line between life and death, I got help, and I got sober. That made all the difference. I can't imagine I would have lived to see 25 without sobriety. Or who else I might have harmed beyond myself.

DA: How did you approach writing such an emotionally charged memoir?

KG: I had those journals I'd kept since I was eighteen years old. But they sunk me. Everything seemed without hope. Even though they had some valuable information—dates, dialogue, etc.——I kept them in another room. Michael Burkard read my very first "draft" of the memoir, which was 350 journal pages cobbled together and lightly edited. While he'd encouraged me with the material, he said, "You haven't written it yet." Of course, he was right, and I had to write it from this point in time. I'd complained to Michael that because no one in my family spoke about my son, I didn't know enough to write the book. But Michael had said, "No, you do know some things." He suggested I start with those. I began with the town of Brockton, where I was born and where my son lived and is buried. Brockton had been a shoemaking town for over 200 years, with 90 shoe factories. I began researching the history of shoes and shoemaking. I couldn't talk to anyone about my son, but I could learn how to make a shoe. I then took a prose workshop with Richard McCann at the Fine Arts Work Center in Provincetown, and I brought my first piece, a rambling essay about many things, including the history of shoes in Brockton. After my workshop, Richard told me, "Think shoes." I went home and wrote about my son and grief in the essay, "How to Make a Shoe." *AGNI* published it, and it received special mention in the *Pushcart Prize* anthology. I felt that I had to approach my subjects from the side, that it would do me no good to write head on. Richard McCann had also said that while he was a fellow at Virginia Center for the Creative Arts, he had a writing studio that was downstairs. As he walked down those stairs to work, he'd think, "Down, Down, In." I thought of that often as I wrote the memoir. It helped me to stop time in scenes and to go down into events I thought I knew. To try to see them from this point in time. I wanted prose with the power of poetry. Prose that can see an unseen world.

DA: You gained invaluable experience with people over the years working at non-profit organizations.

KG: I'd created a literary nonprofit organization while I was a graduate student. Don Stap at UCF had recommended me for a three-week writing residency at Atlantic Center for the Arts in New Smyrna Beach, Florida. I was in residence with Alfred Leslie, Jonathan Williams, Terry Riley and 23 emerging and mid-career artists working in poetry, painting, and music. Living and working within this community of artists changed my life. When I came back to Orlando, I was lonely for that community. I loved attending readings, but there were only a few a year. I was hungry for more, and created liquid poetry out of a desire for something ongoing. Literary events integrated into the every day instead of occasional. In venues that included independent bookstores, university art galleries, and coffee shops, we presented over 100 events in five years —reading series, videotaped author interview series, writing workshops, annual writing contests, and publication opportunities. This volunteer work led me to my first nonprofit employment at an opera company. I knew nothing about opera when I was hired, and it was thrilling to learn and have a whole new world open up. I began as a development assistant and before I left, had been promoted to associate director of development. We presented full-scale productions and also supported the work of young opera singers through year-long residencies and children's programs.

DA: You also worked with a coalition for the homeless.

KG: Yes, In 2002, I joined the Coalition for the Homeless of Central Florida as their director of grants administration. As with the opera, I had no background working with the homeless, or even with social services. Again, it was stepping into a new world. Luckily, the program manager decided my office shouldn't be with other administrative personnel. Instead, my office was a room next to the clients' rooms. I worked where they lived, and I was surrounded by children. Over 200 kids (under 7 years old) lived at the Coalition every day. Children and infants, families, single women, single men—700 people a night, and 300,000 meals served annually. The Coalition had been held up as a national model as it included so many services on-site: case management, job services, day care, education, a children's counselor, alcohol and drug treatment program, transitional housing, and domestic violence shelter (at another location). But they need much more funding support. Those 700 people live in a building that is an old TV station from the 1950s. The men, up to 375 each night, sleep on mats on a cement floor in a metal tent. Last year, the Coalition provided nearly 250,000 nights of shelter. Nearly 80,000 nights of shelter were provided to children under 8 years old. The homeless are often stereotyped, and people often use those stereotypes as an excuse not to help. I'm very grateful for the three years I had at the Coalition.

DA: And now teaching is part of your life again.

KG: Yes, I teach in an amazing low-residency MFA program directed by Brian Turner at Sierra Nevada College, Lake Tahoe. I love teaching and working with other writers, and am very excited for the upcoming residency in August. I also just completed a terrific year as distinguished writer-in-residence at SNC, teaching poetry, fiction, and creative nonfiction workshops to undergraduates. I feel very lucky to be with Brian and the stellar faculty at SNC and to work with such promising new writers.

DA: What's next on the agenda in the life of Kelle Groom?

KG: I'm working on a second memoir and a fourth book of poems. I've also just begun working on a novel. Next Spring, I'm very glad to be in Stonington, CT as the James Merrill Writer-in-Residence.

Published in *Pif Magazine* July 1st, 2013

Poems by Kelle Groom

THE BOY WITH HIS MOTHER INSIDE HIM

You said meet me by the harbor church, tide wall, little beach,
and while I waited I walked into the water, salt in the flare

of my jeans. A light when on in the house next door,
a stranger was farther down the shore, no moon, ocean quiet

with me waiting. When I stood, I felt the darkness of the tar,
and then the darkness of the night, and then you were behind the turn

of my head, behind my one Heidi-ponytail, behind my green
corduroy jacket, the night like a big hat on my head

turned with me to see you.

(Originally in *The New Yorker* and in *Underwater City*, U Press of Florida, 2004)

LOUD HOUSE

Het up boys, skitter boys, muttonchop
go-go boys, gurgle music, kidney stone
music, muchachos party, rubicon sand fire
flaring party, thunderbird ski hats in summer
party, sweaty head party, pound & thump,
socket burning beach party, orange forklift
beach, orange moon ba-boom, hooch smoke,
ta-ta smoke, stonkered house, pandemonium
tetherballed, turtle orbitted, oriflamme ant
house, rust hilled, I know I'm violating
myself house, Maybe you'll see me
on MTV house, No, dude (to a dog) house,
evening knock knock knock knock

house, evening anamatter clink: glass and tin,
goo food jars, chest hammer music, earthmover,
dog bark music, beep beep back-up
talk, rag and straw sleep, panic sleep, dart
sleep, rummage, rumple, canyon sleep,
sulky bunco, mittenheaded boys, saw-
voiced reclamation boys, fumarole,
radio pale, tar breathing boys
in the chewed grass, white sail an exhale.

(Originally published in *32 Poems* and in *Five Kingdoms*, Anhinga, 2010)

Oh dont

   —Albumen silver print attributed to F.M. Parkes & Reeves

the spirit wrote
after the Civil War,
in cloudy script
like you might expect
from someone without
hands, the mediums
busy with so many dead,
collective push
into the other world,
all of us calling.
Down by the river
I remembered sawdust
his guitar, two or three
songs, his hand palm
up, showing me the place
where his mother died,
like a mirror he thought
of his own death, and when
the table turned,
he appeared. We walked

around a fallen tree,
the woman in me still
driving by. His dance
was the best part, I mean
no one was dancing, men
and women in night
outfits. Even broken,
cement to my thigh,
I climbed the stairs
and breathed the way
I did at fifteen, taking
in the burning. One spirit
passed her arm through
a chair, roses, like the ones
he carried to me saying
he'd never sleep again.
There's red in the sky, red
in the table, like winter,
the shining garment that materialized.
Oh dont keep calling?
Oh dont stop?
In another photograph,
a spirit has written *Difficult*
to manifest present conditions
not suitable, and another, in tiny
script, *la porte fermé*—so hard
to see it could be fume, though
the closed door is what I've stared
at so long, when even
a blind girl can see that's smoke.

(Originally published in *Witness* and in *Five Kingdoms*, Anhinga, 2010, anthologized in *Best American Poetry* 2010.)

Julie Kane

Julie Kane's poetry collection, *Jazz Funeral* (Story Line Press), was selected by David Mason as the winner of the 2009 Donald Justice Poetry Prize. Her collection, *Rhythm & Booze* (University of Illinois Press, 2003), was chosen by Maxine Kumin as a National Poetry Series winner and was one of four finalists for the 2005 Poets' Prize.

Kane, a native of Boston and longtime resident of Louisiana, is also a nonfiction writer, an editor, translator, and scholar. Kane served as co-editor, with Grace Bauer, of the anthology *Umpteen Ways of Looking at a Possum: Critical and Creative Responses to Everette Maddox* (Xavier Review Press), one of three finalists for the 2007 Southern Independent Booksellers Alliance Book Award in Poetry.

Photo © Julie Kane

She is also an associate editor of the Longman Southern literature anthology, *Voices of the American South* (2004), a comprehensive survey of pivotal works in the Southern literary tradition, and co-authored, with Kiem Do, the non-fiction Vietnam memoir, *Counterpart* (US Naval Institute Press, May, 1998), a 1999 History Book Club featured alternative.

Her other accomplishments include a Fulbright Scholarship to Vilnius Pedagogical University (Lithuania), an Academy of American Poets Prize, New Orleans Writer-in-Residence terms at Tulane University, and a Pushcart nomination. She has lived in Natchitoches since 1999 and teaches creative writing and poetry at Northwestern State University.

Derek Alger: Did you want to be a poet from an early age?

Julie Kane: Oh, yes. The first day of class every year in grade school, I would always bring my English book home and read every single poem in it that same night. My first poetry publication came when I was seven years old, in the comics section of a Boston Sunday newspaper—they had a little space reserved for poems and artwork by kids.

DA: Your family was Boston Irish Catholic.

JK: All of my great-grandparents came over from Ireland and settled around Boston. My father grew up poor in Somerville and Melrose; his father drove a horse-drawn vegetable cart in Boston's Faneuil Hall Market. My mother was from Foxboro. Her father had managed to get through a two-year business college after service in World War I, he had a low-level management job with the Foxboro Company. They quite literally had lace curtains up on the windows. But my mother was still embarrassed about being Irish. One of her uncles was the town drunk, serenading her friends from his hangout on the Foxboro town common. Her grandmother kept chickens in her front yard. My mother wanted to get the hell out of Foxboro, and my father wanted to succeed as a newscaster, so they both got rid of their accents and the trappings of ethnicity. We moved around a lot when I was a kid, because of my father's career ambitions.

DA: Your father escaped poverty in large part due to the GI Bill.

JK: Growing up, he never paid much attention to school. He liked playing sports, stealing cars and going joyriding with his friends, hanging out at the racetrack. His parents separated, and his father tended to drink up his paycheck rather than provide for his children. My father graduated from high school in 1942 and got drafted into World War II. When he got out, he was able to go to college on the GI Bill. He had the most beautiful bass speaking voice you've ever heard, and he studied broadcast journalism at Boston University and became a radio and TV newscaster.

DA: Your choice to attend Cornell University paid off on many levels. How'd you end up there?

JK: My father was a TV newsman in Binghamton, New York, for about four years when I was in grade school. We took several day trips to Ithaca and the Finger Lakes region, about an hour away—I was stunned by the beauty of the mountains and gorges and glacial lakes. Given that I was applying for colleges at the same time a lot of traditionally male-only universities were finally opening up to women, I was also impressed that Cornell had always admitted women—we weren't going to be patronized there.

It was a stroke of luck that I landed there, because they had an exceptionally lively poetry scene in the early 1970s. A.R. Ammons—"Archie," to us students—and Bill Matthews were both on the faculty then. Bob Morgan came later. Billy Joe Harris was teaching American poetry. You would not believe the students who were there at the same time I was, all of whom have gone on to publish multiple volumes of poetry.

DA: *Try me.*

JK: Okay, here goes. Diane Ackerman; Sharon Dolin; Wendy Battin, a winner of the National Poetry Series; Ken McClane; Cecil Giscombe; Stephen Tapscott, who's become a well-known translator of Spanish-language poetry; James Bertolino; Gilbert Allen; Mark Anderson; John Latta; David McAleavey; Dan Fogel; Judy Epstein.

DA: *Not a bad line-up.*

JK: Lynn Shoemaker was in town, teaching shop at a local school, and Rich Jorgensen, the editor of the 70s little magazine *The Stone*, was running an organic bakery. Gary Esolen was a young assistant dean. It was like The Harmonic Convergence, poetry-wise. There were weekly poetry readings in The Temple of Zeus, a coffee house on campus with life-sized plaster statues of Greek gods, and lots of other readings other places. Ithaca House was in town—publishing letterpress poetry books, and *Epoch*, edited by the Cornell faculty and grad students, was one of the leading lit mags at the time. Wendy Battin was the editor of the "official" Cornell literary magazine, *Rainy Day*, and just to be ornery, Mark Anderson and Gil Allen and I founded an alternative magazine called *Solstice*—we'd type the thing up on a rented IBM typewriter that cost us our beer money for the week. But really, we were all friends, and the atmosphere was so heady, so exciting—we were eating and breathing poetry.

DA: You received early recognition for your poetry.

JK: I won first prize in the *Mademoiselle Magazine* College Poetry Competition while I was at Cornell. Anne Sexton and James Merrill were the judges that year. And then Diane Ackerman took two of my poems for *Epoch* when she was the poetry editor—I was an undergrad and she was in the PhD program, so I was thrilled beyond belief that she considered me a "real poet." T. Corraghessen Boyle, Marilyn Hacker, and Sandra Gilbert all had work in that Winter 1974 issue of *Epoch*. Maybe I'll be able to sell my copy on eBay to fund my retirement.

DA: You had to make quite a choice when it came to grad school.

JK: I got into the Iowa Writers Workshop, which was considered to be the best MFA program at the time—there were only about a dozen of them. But I also got into Boston University, where my idol Anne Sexton was teaching. BU had the aura of being associated with Confessional poetry—Sexton and Plath had taken a course with Robert Lowell there. It wasn't all that long after Plath's death, remember—not much more than a decade. Plath was still pretty much a cult figure then, except to us young women poets, who realized her significance. BU gave me a tuition scholarship; and I had an aunt in Boston who was willing to take care of my cat for a year, because the only apartment I could find in one frantic day of searching did not allow pets. So that all tipped the balance toward BU.

DA: Your experience with Sexton turned out to be rather traumatic.

JK: She committed suicide just four or five weeks into my first semester at BU, in October of 1974. Even today, I can hardly talk about it. We —her students, I mean—just adored her. And she had been upbeat in her last class with us, very excited about a reading in the Midwest that was paying her several thousand dollars. It happened on the weekend, I remember, and my aunt—the one who was keeping my cat—told me at breakfast, because she didn't want me to hear it on the news the way she had. That was not a good year for BU's creative writing faculty. John Cheever crashed and burned alcoholically and couldn't finish out the year—he was admitted to a rehabilitation facility in the spring. But he recovered and got a very fine book out of it, *Falconer*. For the rest of that fall semester, BU kept sending one accomplished poet after another in to substitute-teach Sexton's class, much like sending Christians in to the lions, because we'd just sit there and glare at them: "You're not Anne!" James Tate and others. In the spring, Charles Simic finally took over the graduate poetry seminar. His style was very different from Anne's— he was distant and cool, whereas she'd been so electric and warm—but he was a fine teacher. I couldn't help thinking about the road not taken, though—what if I'd gone to Iowa instead? There was no real reason to be there with Anne gone.

DA: You received another honor after earning your MA in creative writing.

JK: I became the first female George Bennett Fellow in Writing at Phillips Exeter Academy. Exeter had just begun admitting girls as students, and there were only a couple of women on the faculty, so I was the butt of a lot of "fellow" jokes, as you can imagine! It was a lovely little colonial New England town, and the students were very smart and endearing, but I didn't have much to do—all I had to do was write poems and visit English classes when someone invited me. The snow was up to the windowsills and everybody else but me on the faculty was really busy, so I wound up getting married to the guy I was dating at the time. You couldn't really have your boyfriend stay overnight when you were living in an apartment in the middle of a prep school campus.

DA: Your marriage led to a major geographical change.

JK: My husband was from Louisiana. He had transferred to Cornell from Louisiana State University. This was during the Civil Rights era, remember, and he swore that he was never going back to the South. But then he started getting the bug to go to law school like his grandfather and uncle and father—he applied to the Iowa Writers Workshop and to LSU Law School, and got into both, and it was "Two roads diverged" all over again. Iowa gave him a teaching assistantship and then snatched it away because he didn't have previous teaching experience, and LSU started looking better and better. We packed up the cat and our poetry books and moved to Baton Rouge in June, 1976.

DA: How did you end up in New Orleans?

JK: My marriage fell apart while my husband was still in law school, and I was fully expecting to flee back North as soon as possible. But I had been to New Orleans a few times, and I loved what I knew of it—the French Quarter, palm trees, cafe au lait and beignets. I thought, maybe I'll just check out New Orleans for a year or two before I go back home. I answered an ad for a technical writer with Exxon Nuclear—they were managing the procedure production effort for a nuclear power plant under construction upriver from New Orleans. Exxon hired me, and I moved to New Orleans in 1978. At first, I was living on the West Bank, across the river from the city, and later on I moved uptown, to the Carrollton area.

DA: Were you still writing poetry in those years?

JK: Oh, yes. I never stopped. I lost faith in myself for a long while, but I never stopped writing. While I was still living in Baton Rouge, my husband and I belonged to a writer's workshop that had some incredible people in it. Wyatt Prunty, W.S. DiPiero, Charlotte Holmes, William "Kit" Hathaway, Sue Owen. And when I moved to New Orleans, I fell in with a couple of old friends who were poets, and we'd go to readings and talk poetry. Ken Fontenot, whom I'd met in Baton Rouge, was living in New Orleans East. Gary Esolen from Cornell turned up, living in a crumbling boarding house and writing for an alternative newspaper—eventually he would found the weekly *Gambit*. He and I gave readings at The Maple Leaf Bar a couple times in the late 1970s. Gary would bring his dirty laundry with him in a duffelbag and wash and dry it in the machines in the back of the bar—the machines are long gone now. One time Gary took me to a party of New Orleans journalists and I met a British poet named Geoffrey Godbert who edited a little magazine and a small press back in London. We struck up a friendship and began corresponding, and eventually he asked to see my poetry manuscript and I sent it to him, and he took half of it and half of another American woman poet's, and titled the collection *Two Into One*. It was published in London in 1982 by Geoffrey's Only Poetry Press. In 1986, I moved to an apartment just four blocks from the Maple Leaf, and I became a regular at their weekly poetry readings. I became friends with Everette

Maddox, Nancy Harris, Grace Bauer, and other poets connected with "The Leaf."

DA: Then a major turning point in your life occurred.

JK: There were two turning points, really. The first one came in 1987 when two men I knew from the Maple Leaf, Bill Roberts and Hank Staples, decided to start up a small press. Bill and I had dated for a few months in 1985, and he didn't like me very much any more, but he really liked my poetry. Hank was a bartender then and is one of the bar owners now. They published *Body and Soul*, my first full-length book in 1987. Even though it never got distributed much beyond South Louisiana, it gave me new hope that my poems would find their way to readers.

The second turning point came when I gave up drinking in May of 1990. Everette had died homeless and alcoholic the year before, after publishing in *The New Yorker* and *The Paris Review* when he was in his twenties. I didn't want to wind up like him. I could look back and see that my work had enjoyed early success, but that my life had somehow derailed since then, like a train. I was never a daily drinker like Rette, but I was drinking too much on the weekends, and I was starting to experience the consequences. I was afraid, at first, that the sober life would mean giving up my creativity, my spontaneity. After I quit, I began to think more clearly, and I realized that I needed to give poetry my best shot, because it meant more to me than anything.

Some lines from Robert Frost's "Two Tramps in Mud Time" kept haunting me: "But yield who will to their separation, / My object in living is to unite / My avocation and my vocation / As my two eyes make one in sight."

So I resigned from my high-paying tech writing job and enrolled in the Ph.D. program at Louisiana State University, on a $12,000 a year fellowship. I was 39 years old. I was hoping that a literature Ph.D. with a creative writing minor would help get me a college teaching job, and that having a university as a base would make me appear more professional, less amateurish, to editors and other poetry professionals.

Plus, poetry was what I loved to do—I wouldn't be compartmentalizing my life any more, with one box labeled "work" and one labeled "poetry." Still, I'm glad that I was able to work outside of the academy for so many years—I hope that it helped to inoculate me against passing critical fads, to give me more of a sense of the general audience for poetry.

DA: Next stop, a surprise in London.

JK: My old friend Geoffrey Godbert and his friends, Harold Pinter and Anthony Astbury, had founded Greville Press in London, which was publishing beautiful letterpress chapbooks—"pamphlets," as the British call them. Geoffrey and I were still corresponding and sticking new poems in the envelopes, keeping each other up to date on what we were writing. To my surprise, Geoffrey showed some new poems of mine to Harold and Anthony, and he wrote me back that the three of them wanted to publish them as a Greville Press pamphlet. So *The Bartender Poems* came out in the fall of 1991. I was invited to read at the South Bank Centre in London in October, 1991 together with C.H. Sisson, and Harold Pinter introduced the two of us. I felt like Cinderella at the ball—then it was back to Louisiana and life as a lowly and impoverished grad student.

DA: Back to the Ph.D., what was your dissertation about?

JK: It was about the villanelle's transition from a musical genre to a fixed poetic form. Dave Smith directed it. I think I chose that subject because I had begun writing villanelles rather obsessively, and I was concerned about the identification of formal poetry with conservative politics in some people's minds. These days, anyone can choose to write a villanelle one day and a free verse poem the next, but back then, when New Formalism was new, writing in form was weirdly controversial—the choice provoked outrage from some poets and critics. Form, particularly the villanelle, was what felt fresh and exciting to me at the time, but I was worried that I might be deluding myself—was I being anachronistic, not contemporary? I started wondering how a poetic form gets fixed in the first place—what are the circumstances, the politics? It wound up winning the dissertation award at LSU. It was a lot of fun to research, kind of like poetic detective work.

DA: Then you began teaching.

JK: I got my Ph.D. in May 1999 and was hired as a visiting assistant professor at Northwestern State University (in Natchitoches, Louisiana) starting that fall. The plan was that I would launch a national job search while picking up a year of full-time college teaching experience. But they liked me and I liked them, and so the position became permanent.

DA: You also taught in Lithuania.

JK: Yes. During my first year of teaching at NSU, my father fell ill with lung cancer, and then while he was dying, my favorite aunt (the keeper of the cat) died in Boston, and I was named the executrix of her will, and then I was diagnosed with a bad stage of malignant melanoma, and I had surgery in June of 2000. I had a two-and-one-half year waiting period ahead of me to sweat out, during which most melanomas recur if they are going to recur. As you can imagine, I was sort of overwhelmed with intimations of mortality. I decided that I wanted to travel to Lithuania before I died, if I were going to die, because I had made some friends there, poets and a journalist, while it was still part of the Soviet empire, and I had daydreamed for years about visiting them and seeing their fascinating country. (How I made those friends is a long story involving Tipitina's nightclub in New Orleans circa 1988, and a non-English-speaking guy sitting all by himself at a table when my friends and I wanted to put our winter coats on the back of a chair.) So I applied for a Fulbright Scholarship to Lithuania, and I got it, and I taught at Vilnius Pedagogical University in 2002. I love Lithuania. I went back there in 2005 for the Poetry Spring Festival, as a guest of the Lithuanian Writers Union.

DA: While you were there, you got another big break.

JK: My bout with cancer had inspired me to polish up my poetry manuscript and send it out to a dozen or so poetry book contests before I left the country—one last Hail Mary shot. Or maybe "grapeshot" is more accurate. One day in Vilnius, I just happened to look in my junk mail folder, which I didn't always check before deleting stuff, and there was an email message from the National Poetry Series, alerting me that

I was a finalist. They wanted me to rush five copies of my manuscript to them; the address was a P.O. box. I was in a panic—they had pretty strict format rules, and I couldn't even buy 8-1/2 by 11 paper in Vilnius —the paper size there was metric. Plus, I couldn't use any of the private international mail delivery services, because of the P.O. box. Finally, I thought of emailing the manuscript file to my little sister Cindy in New Jersey. She printed it out, ran off four more copies, and mailed it for me. And it won! It was Maxine Kumin's selection for the 2002 competition. *Rhythm & Booze* was published by the University of Illinois Press in 2003. Finally, I had a book out with a nationally distributed press — people were actually going to be able to find it in bookstores or order it online! When I was dealing with the melanoma diagnosis and the thought of possibly dying in the next few years, that had been my one regret, that I had never published a "real" book. There had been several times in my life when I had been faced with a choice between poetry or personal happiness, or poetry and financial security, and I had always chosen poetry—twice when men I loved wanted me to marry them and relocate, but moving would have meant giving up the poetry community at Cornell, or later giving up my creative writing job at NSU. I had to face the fact that I had sacrificed marriage, children, and financial security for poetry, but it looked like maybe my poetry wasn't all that good after all. Ouch.

DA: Fortunately, you didn't have a bad landing.

JK: It's funny: as soon as I let go of my dream, the poetry gods relented and let me have it. Ever since then, good things have been happening. *Rhythm & Booze* was a finalist for the 2005 Poets' Prize. My third book, *Jazz Funeral*, just won the 2009 Donald Justice Poetry Prize, judged by David Mason. Best of all, I've been able to mentor my students and younger writers—to give back what was given so freely to me by my own teachers. F. Scott Fitzgerald once said that there are no second acts in American life, but, yikes, look at me! I've been blessed with second chances.

Published in *Pif Magazine* September 17th, 2009

Poems by Julie Kane

Thirteen

All summer she twirled
in pearls and satin gowns,
pale as a mushroom
in the attic.
Sometimes her aunt or
her father would hint that
the field of Queen Anne's lace
at the end of the road
was chock-full of children
her age. Her age
was suddenly uncertain as
the woman's breath
rising and falling
in an oxygen tent
all summer long.
Nothing to do but wait.
In the stale heat
of the attic, in the rippled
full-length mirror,
she posed
in velvet, in chiffon,
in her mother's useless clothes:
waiting for her breasts
to blossom and fill
the loose bodice of her grief.

Dead Armadillo Song

I've never seen a live
armadillo, but I drive

Route 90, where the shoulder's

littered with the colder,
deader little critters,
getting stiffer and stiffer.

They seem to have weights
like living-room drapes

in their bottoms, for they lie
with their feet to the sky.

By God, there's a lot of 'em,
fat as stuffed ottomans,

World War I tanks snared
in terrorist warfare,

or small coats of armor
whose knights became farmers.

The Mermaid Story

I.

We've all heard half of the fairy tale:
A mermaid rescued a drowning prince,
swam him to shore, then pined away
because she missed the weight of him

and the heat of his breath against her neck;
nothing at all like the trickle of cool
saltwater flushed from delicate gills
when she kissed the mermen back in school.

But since there are witches underwater
as well as over, within a year
she'd bargained away her tail for legs—
and her tongue, too, as legs were dear.

She married the prince. His body hair
tickled like beach grass parched in sun.
An eel grew where his legs forked.
(She couldn't speak this to anyone.)

II.

Back in the anti-universe,
a woman writer with two tongues
rooted to the floor of her mouth
like anemones has just swum

so deep with her freak tail,
the sea spins and her brain goes black.
We'll see if the tongue she bargained for
can send a message back.

Amy King

Amy King is the author of *I'm the Man Who Loves You* and *Antidotes for an Alibi*, both from Blazevox Books, *The People Instruments* (Pavement Saw Press), *Kiss Me With the Mouth of Your Country* (Dusie Press), and most recently, *Slaves to Do These Things* (Blazevox). *I Want to Make You Safe* was published by Litmus Press, 2011.

King teaches English and Creative Writing at SUNY Nassau Community College, located in Huntington, Long Island. Her poems have been nominated for several Pushcart Prizes, and she has been the recipient of a MacArthur Scholarship for Poetry. She was also the 2007 Poet Laureate of the Blogosphere.

In addition to organizing "The Count" and interviews for VIDA: Woman in Literary Arts, King edits the *Poetics List*, sponsored by The Electronic Poetry Center (SUNY-Buffalo/University of Pennsylvania). She also moderates the Women's Poetry Listserv (WOMPO) and the Goodreads Poetry! Group.

King is currently preparing a book of interviews with the poet, Ron Padgett, and is also co-editing *Poets for Living Waters* with Heidi Lynn Staples and *Esque Magazine* with Ana Bozicevic. She also founded and curated the Brooklyn-based reading series, The Stain of Poetry, from 2006 until 2010.

Derek Alger: You were fortunate to run into a perceptive teacher in high school.

Amy King: My English teacher Carolyn Benfer rescued me in a number of ways. I left home at 17, had just begun my senior year of high school and was focused on Surviving. A job closing McDonalds and one working for the Department of Defense, vocational studies in Accounting, and serious lack of sleep didn't exactly draw out my creative proclivities. But she did. First, she encouraged me to enter an essay in a citywide Black History Month contest, and later encouraged me to write a short story for the Baltimore Artscape contest that year. Lucille Clifton judged, selected my story, and then-Mayor Kurt Schmoke delivered my award in public at the courthouse, complete with monetary perk. The essay also won, among others. Ms. Benfer took me to the Channel 2 station herself, where popular news anchor Beverly Burke greeted and gave out, on the 6 o'clock news, the awards.

DA: Do you remember your feelings at the time?

AK: Encouraged, though uncertain about the possibilities of the creative arts. Even in my early college days, my schedule reflected Accounting classes and other surefire means for making money. That mode still sticks in my craw today.

But especially back then, my psyche brewed with a mix of anger and possibility. Anger for the past and issues I hadn't resolved, primarily familial ones, and the possibility that came with escape from circumstance (true life Dickens' tale!) as well as that which accompanies discovery, particularly as I explored the arts.

Literature classes opened onto new worlds, including Gertrude Stein, who thrilled and confounded, as did later friends who were filmmakers, activists and mixed media artists. I had never met such beings in my childhood and was enthralled with how much potential they felt, how free they seemed, the odd things they made and the mediums they used to explore and validate their ideas. I sought out and got to play in the land of art, resisted through the world of protests and political actions, and generally talked with peers who made me feel like I could make things, even out of words.

DA: You decided to continue on to graduate school.

AK: I needed to leave Baltimore. I applied to exactly two grad schools and went to the closest one that accepted me: SUNY Buffalo. I knew nothing of their Poetics program, though I had to choose a discipline to work through (having entered through American Studies), and that was the one. My idea was to find a female poet teaching in the program. I looked in the catalog, went to the English Department and, following the first woman who looked like a professor down the hallway, stopped her and asked, "Are you Susan Howe?" She was and right there agreed to work independently with me. Lucky coincidence. Progressively, I took classes with Charles Bernstein, Carl Dennis, Irving Feldman, Masani Alexis DeVeaux, among other thinking individuals who made me think.

DA: You also gained valuable experience in the working world.

AK: Aside from student loans, I needed cash. I had no family, no money, nada. So I worked at jobs I enjoyed. Again, luck. For three years, I worked as a residence counselor at a home for learning disabled adults. One learns patience in such circumstance, but also empathy. I mean, I entered someone's home on a daily basis and was expected to help the residents in their domestic setting, advocate for them on appointments, and aid them in their work lives. As in any situation, I disliked some and really loved others. Even felt tepid towards a few, but protective. Such is life. But the thing that struck and stuck was recognizing the person in the diagnosis. Because the first thing you learn is a file for each resident. What code they're on. What meds they take. What their diagnoses are. They're labeled from jump.

So I learned that Mike had a head trauma that left him partially paralyzed with negligent short-term memory. He was on yellow code by default of his limitations. Paul had sexual proclivities that were illegal when actualized. He was on red code. Cory was overweight, had epilepsy and subsequent health issues but was on green code. And so the list goes for 12 – 14 residents at a time. What you don't realize is that Michael is hilarious and sassy when he wants his way. He also croons oldies when he's feeling fine. Paul can charm, talk politics, help other residents at will, and has an array of generous facets the 'sexual deviant' label masks. On the flip with his green code status, Cory would fondle Lynn if left alone in a room long enough.

I enjoyed my time at the home, navigating through with so many people who were also learning how to live in close proximity to any number of others. Hell, people without such diagnoses would have issues living in such close quarters. The people in whose home I worked did well to get along most of the time, interact and sometimes even enjoy the company—and not hate the revolving roster of counselors that changed on a regular basis. I don't like when a substitute delivery guy leaves my boxes in the wrong spot, let alone when twelve people occupy the three bathrooms in the house.

DA: Was that the only job that sticks out?

AK: Oh, I thrilled to my job as a medical secretary in Labor & Delivery at Children's Hospital in Buffalo. I'm not sure I should have, but I did. It was a high-risk hospital, so we saw lots of patients, had loads of resident doctors rotating through, and heralded many long-term reputable docs. The nurses were maybe the best, though. Once in, they made a career of it. They were like a family, with loads of seniority, and I learned a lot just from hanging out, listening in. They had means for resisting bad calls doctors made; they compared notes and knew which docs were the real deal. Sometimes they seemed to know more than anyone else on the floor. And overall, the nurses were the most empathetic and attentive group—consistently—with the patients on that floor. Just observing them was an experiential pleasure.

DA: And after Buffalo?

AK: I stayed a year longer than my studies required. Then the question: Atlanta or New York City? If Atlanta, then likely never NYC. But if NYC, then easy right turn to Atlanta. So I left with a then-friend for Williamsburg, Brooklyn in the midst of what seemed like a mass exodus of others from Buffalo to Brooklyn. *Utne Reader* also about that time declared my new neighborhood the hip spot to move to. That ruined it later (see cost of 'artist' lofts from 13 years ago to now).

The city thrilled, though. I loved the energy, the vastness, the arts in spades, the various accents, the dirt, the clash of unplanned architecture, how scenesters eclipsed but artists could be found on the right beer swilling night in some seedy, cheap bar, etc. I loved it. I'm sure everyone has their 'back in the day' NYC stories, but they're real regardless of the numbers. 'Back in my day' Williamsburg was still not quite gentrified and things were still affordable if one worked a regular day job. I think I started my first one at the official Olympic film company making 26K per year, a ton of money to me then. I got to dress as I saw fit, leave by five, and hit the streets for shows and chats and parties and the like, taking it all in on the nightly. I didn't bother with the poetry scene for years and lost touch with a number of Buffalo people. The explorations took me elsewhere, again, to film and video and music. I needed that after the 'closeness' of the Buffalo program.

DA: The poetic voice was still calling.

AK: Yes, in fact, I didn't feel like I wrote as much as I wanted in Buffalo. The program there offered lots of theory and I was likely a little too preoccupied with full-time work as well as being too naive to engage as deeply as I would liked to have in retrospect. I observed, listened in and learned, though. I still wanted to write once in NYC, but again because I was working full-time, felt that I needed structured time and more instruction. MFA programs suddenly had appeal and not in the "I want to get one and teach" way, but in the "class time with knowledgeable instructors giving advice" way. So I kept working and got into Brooklyn College and the New School. I couldn't decide, so I went to both simultaneously one semester while still working my full-time gig. It turned out that Brooklyn College—then—offered more in the way of community feel and also had independent study each semester built in. The New School didn't. I carried on at Brooklyn with the benefit of a much, much cheaper bill.

DA: Did you find yourself concentrating on any special form of poetry?

AK: My Buffalo upbringing held sway still, so I played at the political value of language but was also drawn to a variety: New York School, confessional, etc. I realized, though, despite the usually commercial push to 'find a voice,' that I needn't align myself with any label. With that recognition in place, I continue to explore and write by whatever means feel appropriate for my aims or circumstantial predilections.

DA: You've been lucky to meet and study with many exceptional, as well as encouraging, writers and poets.

AK: Yes, I've studied under, met and even sought out some poets of wonder like the ever-encouraging Elaine Equi, the multifaceted and motivating Ron Padgett, the friendly genius Tomaž Šalamun, and just too many to note, including poets who are my peers in years, and poets on the page or through the Internet I've not come face to face with yet.

DA: You eventually found the right teaching position.

AK: I wasn't actually looking to teach. I worked for an ESL school in Manhattan and enjoyed a good bit of the job, including the international travel. However, the wages hurt as the cost of living rose over the years. After teaching adjunct at Brooklyn College, I decided to throw out a few CVs and wait for them to land. I got a call on the first one I sent. At the interview, I had nothing to lose, figuring this was my first try and would be good practice. I'm still at Nassau Community College in Long Island eight years later and also teach adjunct in Queens. When I got tenure, I moved to Huntington, LI, Walt Whitman's birthplace. My courses range from basic comp classes to Film & Lit, Modern American Poetry, various creative writing courses, etc. The variety each semester, plus the more relaxed setting complete with trees and room to run around, keeps me happy out here. I never thought I would give up my Brooklyn street cred, but I'm faring rather well amongst the birds by the beach now. My more rural southern roots are showing.

DA: You also teach Introduction to Children's Literature.

AK: That, too, was a fluke. I was asked to cover an empty section when I first started, so I made a go of it. I studied and read and tried out a couple of different standard textbooks and finally found my own way into this course. Through trial and error, I've managed to fashion a curriculum that other professors in the department have since adopted. I never would've thought I could teach such a course, except the more I read, the more I realized that the lines between "adult" and "children's" literature are tenuous, flexible and sometimes meant only to protect adults. That, plus a focus on the pleasures of reading, has shaped my focus in the course.

DA: You recently embarked on a new project.

AK: Ana Bozicevic and I finally handed over the reins of our Brooklyn-based reading series, The Stain of Poetry (http://stainofpoetry.wordpress.com), to a few younger energetic NYC poets so that we could focus on other poetic endeavors such as our new magazine, *Esque* (http://www.esquemag.com), and our own writing. Esque was conceived as a way to get more unusual or nontraditional poetry and poetics statements into the world:

Oetry is the kitchen sink, Ifesto is everything but.

Oetry includes the texts of your native turf: poems, prose poems, verse-fragments, visual po-work. Send us especially work you thought was too strange, too out-there or in-here, a/typical, (not-)you, overly bold or bald – just too-something to send elsewhere.

Ifesto is a field for poets to lucidly engage beyond their poetry. It may include: manifestos, rants, theoretical or personal essays, half-formed statements of poetics, travelogues, music or literary or art critiques, a recurring dream. We invite you to write something especially for us: define or fracture the -etics, -eerness, -ility, -onality, -ism you write from or despite of.

Additionally, I have been working with Heidi Lynn Staples on "Poets for Living Waters" as an ongoing response to the Gulf Oil Spill and the continued fallout from Hurricane Katrina. We have readings coming up at AWP and many have happened all over the U.S. Some of these are documented on our site, http://poetsgulfcoast.wordpress.com. In addition to the activism, we're also working with a number of people who use poetry as therapy. More info via Poets and Writers – http://www.pw.org/content/poets_act_on_oil_spill?cmnt_all=1.

Finally, I recently joined the great troupe of women known as VIDA: Women in the Literary Arts to conduct interviews with writers and point out gender imbalances in the publishing world. It has been a pleasure feeling supported and energized as we query the mechanics of publishing – http://vidaweb.org.

DA: You have been credited by many for working tirelessly promoting poetry for communities far and wide.

AK: I don't know that I work tirelessly, but I certainly think anyone who feels entitled to critique a community they belong to should feel just as responsible for shaping that community. That is to say, if I want to see different readings or work published in the world, why should I sit around only complaining about what exists? I can use that same energy to put a little something into the world, or to change that world by asking questions and speculating on causes and solutions. The former effort birthed Stain and Esque and Poets for Living Waters, while the latter is how VIDA supports the changing face of publishing. If we don't identify disparities and bias, then how can we ask questions? And if we don't ask questions, how can we get folks to notice that, say, oh this major publication seems to only interview men with the occasional woman appearing in token fashion?

I do other things, too, that feel relatively minor at this point like moderating the Poetics Listserv (http://epc.buffalo.edu/poetics/welcome.html) as well as WOMPO – Women's Poetry Listserv (http://lists.ncc.edu/scripts/wa.exe?A0=WOM-PO). This work doesn't require much effort as I participate in these communities daily anyway. One can learn so much from just listening in, and when you have a question about poetics or women's poetry, no Internet search engine can replicate the wealth of information the members of these communities respond with. They are truly a priceless, collective resource and, for some who live in more isolated places, a necessary consistent community of supportive writers.

Overall, what I get from this work far surpasses any tired feelings that seldom occur. I stay connected with writers by running a reading series or editing a magazine, and in the process, get to hear new work, feel envious and inspired by it and run back home to my writing desk. The work is regenerative and creative and worth the extra time I have that would likely go into watching movies if it wasn't there to be done.

Published in *Pif Magazine* January 1st, 2011

Poems by Amy King

Butterfly the Gnarled

Into my stomach an explosion of stars
where I rely on myself, my government name, bony letters
of fingers that tunnel your bisected heart, skyward with dark.

Parasites bed my inner lining—
Am I not the rubberized universe?
I am its buffer and get to name things for what they are,
who they serve—what order.

A plural centipede burrows outbound,
crawls the spine of my hand,
tells my pencil to move along, give out lead.
Months of illness do that to a puppet,
gnaw at her strings, place moths on her neighbors,
blend them with gypsies who live the treetops uprooted.

Dare the deliberately happy to butterfly the gnarled roots of life—

That we pass too many pounds of flesh uncut.
Too much genius hermitted in stereo.
The round tables forgetting their bird seed.
Clovers push luck to surround these hollow legs.

Why no windows on the sides of houses?
Why no flames beneath stones that burn?
Why do all minutes lead the blue carp and black eel now?

We'll be passing through heaven in a split pea shell,
emptied of light, hard as effusive green
ore the blood corrupts daily, within and without.

from *I Want to Make You Safe*. Copyright © 2011 by Amy King. Reprinted by permission of Litmus Press.

Some Pink in Your Color

Did you know I'm in this hospital bed?
I'm not. I'm in the same light you stand in,
much the same way I'm in the waist of your Carolina
watching from the screen across the bed
whose pulse is worn down with an IV to the head.

We are all snow birds atop
the cherry blossoms of August.
Springtime in Washington D.C.
passed too fast, nearly in the flash of Rose
brushing her teeth over the bedpan.

No adrenal gland has known such cortisol,
such heartbreaking I love you O my God,
so many soldiers on the brink of their lives returning!
Are we still talking to the same god?

I can't imagine the heart anymore
now that it presses my ribs apart,
a balloon of such gravity I ache for stars in a jar,
wasps whose love reminds me of fireflies tonight.

from *I Want to Make You Safe*. Copyright © 2011 by Amy King. Reprinted by permission of Litmus Press.

The Gilded Zero

Only open homes & woods & pansies' blue ledges
can lead the zero with his only arms
to embrace himself in open fields for all to gape upon.
He unbuttons steel-gray sheets, a knotted top coat,
bares himself, his hole, a vision
as framed by the marker that is
where
his body blew and left enclosure intact,

skeletal innards
enough to make moviegoers ask,
"Has anyone finished themselves yet?"
I haven't. I swim the lagoon, take note:
the babies are barely dirty,
their armpits smooth with silky soot
weighted in apartment cycles like
we keep movement in boxes for thunderstorms,
and the railroad leaves a dancing behavior
absorbed by every second thought,
escaping the socket that was his mission,
his body incomplete, to help us
to the maidenhead of Niagara,
a target awakening
the chlorophyll of trees,
their tongues the densest forest
canopy and floor
thigh deep with root rot we sleep on and fold
into growing-whole sheep what becomes of the lot:
night's zero hour
of what is & what isn't, till death, not us part.

from *I Want to Make You Safe*. Copyright © 2011 by Amy King. Reprinted by permission of Litmus Press.

Gloria Mindock

Gloria Mindock is the author of the poetry collections, *Blood Soaked Dresses* (Ibbetson St. Press, 2007), *Nothing Divine Here* (U Šoku Štampa, 2010), and *La Porțile Raiului* (Ars Longa Press, Romania, 2010), translated into the Romanian by Flavia Cosma. Gloria is the editor and publisher of Červená Barva Press, and in 2007, became the editor of the *Istanbul Literary Review*, an online journal based in Turkey. Recently, Gloria became one of the USA editors for *Levure littéraire* in France.

Photo by Zoia Krastanova

Mindock is also the author of three poetry chapbooks, *Doppelganger* (S. Press) *Oh Angel* (U Soku Stampa), and *Pleasure Trout* (Muddy River Books, 2013). Her poems have been published in numerous journals, including *River Styx, Phoebe, Poesia, and Poet Lore, Muddy River Poetry Review, City Lit Rag, UNU: Revistă de Cultură, Gând Românesc, Citadela, Vatra Veche,* to name a few, as well as appearing in several anthologies. Her work has been translated and published into the Romanian, Serbian, French, Spanish and Estonian.

She has had nominations for the Pushcart Prize, St. Botolph Award, and was awarded a fellowship from the Massachusetts Cultural Council distributed by the Somerville Arts Council. From 1984-1994. Mindock edited the Boston Literary Review/Blur and was co-founder of Theatre S & S Press, Inc. During its existence, Theatre S. received grants from the Polaroid Foundation, The Rockefeller Foundation, The Globe Foundation, New England for the Arts, and the Massachusetts Cultural Council. Her poetry collection, *Doppelganger*, served as the text for theatre piece of the same name performed by Theatre S.

Červená Barva Press has received grants from the SUR Translation Program from Buenos Aires, Argentina to publish a translation from Luis Raul Calvo and recently from CLD Larentides in Quebec, Canada, to publish Les cahiers de Val-David Festival Notebooks/Los cuadernos de Val-David 2009-2014 Anthologie brève.

Over the years, Mindock has performed, acted, composed music, and sang in the theatre. Her most recent performance piece was "Walking In El Salvador." Mindock lives in Somerville, MA, where she works as a social worker, does freelance editing of manuscripts, and conducts workshops for writers in her Červená Barva Press studio at the Center for the Arts at the Armory.

Derek Alger: Were you creative as a kid?

Gloria Mindock: I was always creative as a kid. I wrote music all the time and words to go with it. I remember one song about the Mississippi River when I was 10 years old. I still remember it! As I got older, I still loved music but I turned to acting and theatre. I acted in plays in high school. My senior year in high school, the drama department was started again by Mr. Gordon Rogers. I thought he was remarkable. He called me "Little Nutsy." I ended up acting in *The Skin Of Our Teeth* by Thornton Wilder in college that he directed. I had a blast. He had a deep voice and could recite Shakespeare for hours. It was amazing. He was such an inspiration to me. He died some years ago which was a real loss.

I also did a few plays at St. Bede High School in Peru. IL. At that time it was an all-guy Catholic school. My best memory is being in a play that Father Placid Hatfield and Father Gabriel directed. They both were so wonderful and I have never forgotten them. Two very special priests. I often wonder where they are now. I also sang in musicals so it was a great experience.

DA: You originally hailed from the midwest.

GM: Yes, a proud midwesterner, born in LaSalle, Illinois, and raised in Oglesby, population 3,800. I disliked high school except for a few teachers. I had great friends throughout school. My closest friends from home are Janie, Shirley, Carol, and Sandy. There is a special bond of friendship that will always be. I look forward to going home and spending time with them and my family. My wonderful friends made school bearable, and we had such great times!

DA: And after high school?

GM: I belonged to Stage 212 in LaSalle, IL and was cast as a Kit Kat Girl, Maria, in Cabaret. I loved that musical. I was one of the lead dancers and singers. The cast was great. I went to Illinois Valley Community College for two years just to get the general studies out of the way. Mr. Jim Jewell, who was the lead in Cabaret, was a teacher there. I did many Readers Theatre productions with him as the instructor and had him for a few classes. He was a gem, also like Gordon Rogers. During my community college years, I continued to do theatre. I was very lucky to have such good influences. Other than that, I didn't care for my classes there. I was bored by them. I never believed in studying things that I would never ever use in my life. I am a total radical against the educational system as it stands now and how it was then.

DA: No argument from me.

GM: I went to two other colleges in Illinois and majored in theatre. First, Theatre Education, then Comprehensive Theatre. The department was a nightmare for me and I did not belong there. The teachers were on an ego trip. One semester they knew you, the next, they did not. Some of them seemed jealous of the students. Of course there were some really wonderful teachers but the majority . . . I hated my classes. I did a lot of acting in shows and loved it. Many of them directed by students. This was a wonderful experience and I learned a lot. In the department, at the time, were really great students who were so gifted. You see them today on the big screen and on TV—Jeff Perry, John Malkovich, Terry Kinney, Laurie Metcalf, Rhondi Reed, Gary Cole, and many more. I didn't really know any of them very well. Every student there was talented and so nice.

    I have nothing but good things to say about the students. Real gems! Some of them went on to Steppenwolf Theatre in Chicago, started by Gary Sinise, and then some continued on their career path elsewhere. I have no contact with anyone in the theatre department. I left my mark though and co-directed *Godspell* and it was one of the best attended shows ever. That was in the '70s. So in summary, pertaining to the classes, I was not a model student, but I do not feel bad about this.

DA: Probably prepared you well for other things.

GM: After I left there, I went to another college and majored in Social Work. It was a good fit for me. I wanted to work with addicts. I focused on addictions, criminology, and crisis intervention. I loved it! I had some great teachers. I did grad work in theater and that was a great experience. I liked the teachers. They really cared about their students learning.

DA: You decided to go East after college and ended up co-founding Theatre S. & S Press, publishing books and producing experimental plays.

GM: I moved east to Somerville, Massachusetts and found a home, and a vibrant artistic community. I love theatre, acting is in my blood. What can I say? I love it. At Theatre S, we did original plays and adaptions. We received grants in the 1980's. It was a good time for that. I had some wonderful experiences here working with David Miller, a wonderful performance artist, director, and writer, and Paul Miller, who did film-making at that time, both just brilliant, and so many other wonderful people. It was tons of hard work but worth every minute of it. Even when some of the actors didn't take some things seriously, I still loved it. Yes, I'm old school. I believe in warm-ups and knowing your lines.

DA: Your poetry collection, Doppelganger, *was the text for a piece performed by Theatre S.*

GM: For this collection, Edgar Allen Poe/William Wilson was an inspiration for writing such dark poetry. It was such a thrill seeing it being performed. The set was done to give the feel like you were looking in the windows of a house. The audience had to walk around looking in the windows to see the action and hear the text, which was my poetry.

DA: When did you start writing poetry.

GM: When I was studying theatre at the college talked about previously. I would go into the library and browse the poetry shelves. There I discovered Keats, Shelly, Byron, Matthew Arnold, and some others who I just loved. I was hooked. I also grew up with poetry books around by Frost, Burns, and some others that my mother and dad had.

I wrote mostly plays but in 1982, while my ex-husband was part of the Iowa Writer's Workshop, I started to write poetry. I wrote some pretty bizarre poems. Later, I discovered Eastern European writers and that totally is my inspiration for writing now. One of my very first poems was nominated for a Pushcart Prize. I was floored.

DA: You still had a calling for acting.

GM: Always. I plan on performing a piece called "Walking in El Salvador," which focuses on the atrocities committed there from 1980-1992. It goes along with my book *Blood Soaked Dresses*. Though I haven't done anything in years, I will do this.

DA: *Your poetry collection* Blood Soaked Dresses *has been praised as "a beautiful, harrowing" book.*

GM: This book is very special to me. I worked with Salvadoran refugees who fled the civil war which lasted from 1980-1992. This book is their account of the atrocities and what they told me written in the first person. A follow-up book, *Whiteness of Bone* is almost completed. I had to write about this because the world seems to turn its back on such atrocities and genocide. I wanted to focus on being a voice for the people of El Salvador in this book.

I have always been political following the news of the world. A priest brought El Salvador to my attention. I started hearing so much about it and how could I not get involved? I hope someday they make Arch Bishop Oscar Romero a saint. He was very special to the people of El Salvador. It seemed like at first, he followed what the church told him, and then later, he was there completely for the people.

DA: In 2005, you embarked on another major project.

GM: Yes, I founded Červená Barva Press. It means "Red Color" in Czech. A few friends told me that I couldn't do this and that it would be too much for me. I replied, "Watch me!" So the press was born. We publish chapbooks and books of poetry, fiction, plays, translations, poetry postcards, broadsides, and some non-fiction from writers all over the world. William J. Kelle is the other half of the press. He designs the book covers, websites, chapbooks, and so much more. William is good at what he does. I also have many interns from surrounding colleges help me which has been wonderful.

DA: You also have a pretty demanding job.

GM: Being a social worker/counselor has been wonderful. I work with men age 21 and older in a halfway house in Somerville. I work at a community-based non-profit organization founded in 1970 in response to the growing need for substance abuse treatment. I have worked there since 1984. I like helping clients learn to live sober and get their lives together. They have lost everything in their life due to heroin, alcohol, cocaine, oxy's, and the list goes on, but these are the main drugs of choice. My experiences has all been good. A few times I had rough days on the job but when you look at the whole picture, it has been worth it. So many clients who have come through the program have died. We all try to give them hope. The program is based on AA principles.

DA: What drew you to a specialty in addiction?

GM: I just always believed in helping the less fortunate. My philosophy is that we are all on this planet together. How some people cannot be passionate is beyond me. I volunteered in grade school at a hospital with my friend Jane. We were called, Angelets. At feeding time, we used to hide on the roof because when I fed one patient, he later died. We were freaked out about that. Later in life, and much older, I volunteered for the Red Cross, Kidney Foundation, Easter Seals, and at Anna State Hospital.

DA: Should I ask if you ever sleep.

GM: No.

DA: An email exchange provided you with another creative opportunity.

GM: Yes, I started to correspond with Elkin Getir, the owner, founder, and editor of the *Istanbul Literary Review*. He had the same vision I have. This vision is to bridge the gaps in writing between countries. After corresponding for awhile, Etkin asked me to edit the Istanbul Literary Review. I said yes and was so excited. I started in September, 2007.

DA: How often does the Istanbul Literary Review *come out?*

GM: We publish three issues a year online. Elkin has given me full control of what I choose for the magazine. He trusts me completely with it. Guluzar is the Webmaster, Halime, always puts up the best Turkish recipes each issue, and there is a staff which is quite wonderful.

DA: What can we look for in the future?

GM: Personally, my book, *Whiteness of Bone*, and many new books by Červená Barva Press. In the future, I will publish mostly from European countries.

Published in *Pif Magazine* July 1st, 2011

Poems by Gloria Mindock

EL SALVADOR, 1983

Somewhere, someone is mourning for the
body of a brilliant one.
Man or woman, it doesn't matter.
The tears in this country, an entrance
to a void… shadows touching skin like frost.

A star fell north of this city. Armies parade around
in their uniforms bragging about the killings.
Dead bodies thrown into a pit, cry. Flesh hits wind, wind hits flesh.
How many dead? Finally, they are covered with dirt at noon.
All eyelids are closed.

No one knows nothing.
No breathing assaults to hold us. The bitter ash
weeps over the world, and no other country
wants to see it, tastes the
dead on their tongue or wipe away all
the weeping sounds.

from *Blood Soaked Dresses*

SUITCASE

What shall be packed in my
suitcase when I leave?...
Fairy tales for a life not
lived right.
A whole life of occasional
hearts shoved into a box with
locks. I'm the only one with the
exact memories of all the men I loved.

In one sentence, I can tell you
how many, but why bother. It's none
of your business. Besides, they are going
berserk in there.
I am ever-changing...clumsy.

Wounded and bloodstained on my pale skin, there
is no cure for when the torpedo hits.
Blasting a union into war, I drown at the
mercy of a song.

I should have found shelter.
I take this suitcase with me,
remember my anguish...the love I
grabbed in haste.

from *Nothing Divine Here*

Mark Statman

Mark Statman's most recent books are the poetry collection, *A Map of the Winds* (Lavender Ink, 2013), and *Black Tulips: The Selected Poems of Jose Maria Hinojosa* (University of New Orleans Press, 2012). [His new book of poems, *That Train Again*, will be came from Lavender Ink in April 2015.] He is also the author of the poetry collection, *Tourist at a Miracle* (Hanging Loose, 2010), as well as a translation, with Pedro Medina, of Federico Garcia Lorca's *Poet in New York* (Grove, 2008).

His other books include *Listener in the Snow* (Teachers & Writers, 2000) and, with Christian McEwen, *The Alphabet of the Trees: A Guide to Nature Writing* (Teachers & Writers, 2000). His poetry, essays, and translations have appeared in such publications as *The Cincinnati Review*, *The Florida Review*, *South Dakota Review*, *Tin House*, *Washington Square*, and *American Poetry Review*, to name some of his numerous publications.

Statman is an Associate Professor of Literary Studies at Eugene Lang College of The New School in Manhattan. He is a recipient of awards from the National Endowment for the Arts and the National Writers Project.

Derek Alger: Your most recent poetry collection was prompted by a question asked by your son.

Mark Statman: Yes, this happened when Jesse was a toddler, barely able to look out our kitchen window which looked out into the backyards of our block in Brooklyn. He turned to me and said, Dada, write me a poem called "A Map of the Winds." The poem that appears in the book is actually the second version of the poem. The first coincides with a sense of my own idea of futility—that I couldn't. The second, I think is much more positive. Instead of thinking that it wasn't my poem to write, I thought about how happy I was that this was something he thought I could do. So it became a poem about father and son and a little bit about life in Brooklyn. It was also kind of extraordinary to me in the sense that he already knew I was a poet, that there was such a thing as poetry.

Jesse, and my wife Katherine, and the life we live, whether we are in Brooklyn or upstate or Mexico or wherever, have always inspired me to write. Though Jesse, now that he is twenty, doesn't really travel with us much anymore. He's a musician, has a lot of his own work to do. Still, memory speaks into the poems as present.

DA: Poet John Yamrus described your poems in A Map of the Winds *as delivering "Just good, solid poetry that keeps getting better."*

MS: John Yamrus is a poet for whom I have a great deal of respect. I just wrote the introduction for his book of poems, *Alchemy*, which is coming out in March with Epic Rites Press. I was pleased when he suggested that my work keeps getting better.

I do think *A Map of the Winds* is my best work to date and I am grateful to Bill Lavender at Lavender Press for publishing it. Bill is a terrific publisher. When he was director of the University of New Orleans Press, he accepted my translation collection *Black Tulips: The Selected Poems of Jose Maria Hinojosa* in 2012 as part of their Engaged Writers Series. This was the first English language translation of this significant and lost poet of Spain's Generation of 27, which included Garcia Lorca (whose *Poet in New York* I had translated with Pablo Medina a few years earlier).

A Map of the Winds took me about three years to write. I had published *Tourist at a Miracle* and that is a very coherent and cohesive book. Donna Brook was a terrific editor on it. But there were a lot of poems that were left out. I was also so inspired by the process of working with her that I kept writing new poems, and these seemed to be going in a different direction. They seemed both more domestic and yet more about being someplace else. They were also personal, despite a kind of other quality. I think the idea of the map is a central idea. I'm reminded of Dick Gallup's wonderful book of poems *Wherever I Hang My Hat is Home.*

DA: A lot of work seems to have gone into your poetry.

MS: I am a tireless reviser, every poem gets six or seven drafts. I am still not sure any poem is really done.

DA: I can relate to that.

MS: For *A Map of the Winds*, I am also indebted to Pablo Medina, John Yarmus, and Joseph Lease for giving the manuscript close readings. Joseph Lease, in particular, was a great editor for me. He went through the manuscript, suggested major cuts (of some 60 pages) and that I change the opening poem from "window box" to "promised" (so "window box" becomes the second poem). I think it was a great move because it sets the tone for the rest of the collection. I think "window box" would have suggested a whole different book.

DA: Tell us a bit more about Jose Maria Hinojosa.

MS: *Black Tulips* is the first English translation of Jose Maria Hinojosa. He's a poet I discovered while working on the Lorca book. His name kept appearing in narratives but I couldn't find any of his work. Then I found a small website in Spain that had some of his poems and I thought these are pretty good. I showed them to Pablo (Medina), who I first met when we were both teaching at Lang—he is now at Emerson —and he said, I think you have your next book. But the work was hard to find. Fortunately, I was able to get in touch with the family in Spain who put me in touch with Alfonso Sanchez Rodriguez, the editor of Hinojosa's *Obra Completa* in Spain. He was a great guide.

One of the reasons Hinojosa has not been known in the English-speaking world is that he was barely known in Spain for many years. He was very much a part of the Generation of 27 but he did a curious thing. Andre Breton, in his second *Surrealist Manifesto*, suggests that if you are not a communist, you can't be a surrealist. So Hinojosa goes and visits Stalin's Soviet Union. He is so horrified when he comes back that while all his friends are going left, he goes right. In fact, after that visit in 1928, he writes one more book (his sixth), published in 1931, and then devotes himself to working against the Republic. He wasn't a fascist, more of a Catholic and monarchist. He is murdered in 1936, by forces on the left, three days after Lorca is murdered by forces on the right. There isn't any known connection, but it shows how strange and terrible those times could be.

DA: Why were you drawn to Hinojosa's poetry?

MS: I should start by saying Hinojosa and I have nothing in common politically, but his work is hardly political (save for his final poems). He is a wonderful poet, one of the country, and one of the imagination. He has a great sense of the strange and unusual, poems of place and time. He is a fine love poet and he has a sly sense of humor. As his work develops, he becomes, as did many of the poets of his generation, a voice that was willing to forego the "I" in order to describe the world in ways that were creative and prophetic.

DA: You learned Spanish while growing up.

MS: It's hard for me to describe how I learned Spanish. I heard it a lot growing up. My family on my father's side came from Eastern Europe to Cuba and then the United States, In fact, my great grandparents are buried in Havana. So on that side of my family, the first language was Spanish, second language was Yiddish, and third was English. I think I have a good ear for languages in general, so though I never actually studied Spanish formerly, it seemed natural to me to understand it.

DA: Looks like Brooklyn is your true home.

MS: I was raised in Queens and on Long Island, and then left Long Island when I was 18 to go to Columbia. Other than some time traveling and several years living in the Virginia piedmont, I have been a New Yorker. When Katherine and I left Virginia in 1985 to return to New York, we decided to live in Brooklyn. It seemed like there was a lot of creative energy there. And it was cheaper! Over the years, I've also found it has a spirit that comes out of Walt Whitman, inspiring and rich. I learned a number of years ago that the land that my home on Long Island had originally been owned by the Whitman family. Maybe there's a connection there?

    A thing I love about Brooklyn is its diversity—racial, ethnic, cultural. I love its architecture, its sprawl. I love Manhattan but it doesn't have the same feel, at least, not for me, and not, I think, anymore. After almost thirty years here, I would say it is home.

DA: Did you have an early interest in writing?

MS: Yes. The first poem I ever wrote was "call me Ishmael said the crab / call me fishmeal said Ahab."

But seriously, in high school, I became interested in writing, only my first poems were terrible. I had no idea what I was doing. I showed them to a close friend who was considered the "school poet." This was just before an open reading at my high school. They were so bad that out of kindness she said she had lost them!

I think I became a little more thoughtful about poetry after that, though it wasn't until I got to college that I thought that poetry might be something that would be a major part of my life.

DA: You graduated from Columbia University?

MS: Yes, in 1980. I was very lucky, Columbia was my first choice for college, but I didn't have the money to go. Still I showed up, hoping something might happen. The first week I was there I learned I had received a Joseph Murphy Fellowship, which would cover my tuition for my full four years and allow me to keep other outside scholarships I had received. I majored in Comparative Religions even though I knew literature was where I was going. But I wanted to study something outside of what was comfortable. Interestingly enough, this gave me the chance to study with two of our best translators from eastern religions, Burton Watson and Barbara Stoler Miller.

I did take some courses in the English Department. One was with David Shapiro, who first published at the age of 13 and has written some 20 volumes of poetry. This was a course that was supposed to be about John Keats, and we did read a lot of Keats, but David is so brilliant, everything was fair game. His mind moves faster than anyone I have ever met.

I also studied writing with Kenneth Koch, taking several classes with him. Kenneth was a huge influence on my poetry, and he still is. The funny thing is when I was a senior in college, I introduced Kenneth and Ron Padgett at a reading they were giving at Columbia. There was a young woman with Kenneth and he said, "This is my daughter Katherine." I had a girlfriend at the time and thought nothing of it except, great, he has a daughter. Two years later, Katherine and I were married. And thirty-one years later, we still are. Over the course of time, my relationship with Kenneth went from being student, to younger poet, to son-in-law, to close friend. I still think about him almost every day.

DA: You decided not to follow the MFA path.

MS: There was talk of going for an MA/PhD. I mean, I considered becoming an academic but I'm not sure I knew then what that actually meant. Pablo Medina and I were once reading from Lorca together and I said something like, "Let me get academic here for a second." And Pablo looked at me and said, "Are you an academic?" I answered, "No, I'm a poet." The funny thing is that I've been teaching in academia for decades, as has Pablo.

DA: Seems like a good moment to ask about how your collaboration with Pablo Medina on a translation of Federico Garcia Lorca's work from his time in New York came about.

MS: Pablo and I decided to translate Lorca's *Poet in New York* shortly after the attacks of September 11. Pablo was still teaching at Lang—we were good friends—and it turned out that independently, as part of an attempt to make sense of what had happened, both of us were reading *Poet in New York*. For some crazy reason we decided to translate a few of the poems. *Tin House* published some of those, as did *American Poetry Review*. Grove decided to give us a contract to do the whole book, which we learned was unusual. Translators don't usually get advances on books that haven't been translated! But this was Lorca, after all.

Interestingly enough, though *Poet in New York* is considered in Spain to be one of the greatest works ever written by a Spaniard, it had only been translated into English in its entirety two times before. We soon found out why. If we had known how difficult it was going to be, I'm not sure we'd have accepted the contract! But that we were two friends, two poets, working closely, made it a lot easier. John Ashbery, very kindly, called it "the definitive version of Lorca's masterpiece."

DA: You've been fortunate to travel extensively.

MS: When I was growing up, my family would travel a lot, mainly along the east coast of the United States and in Canada. So I always loved travel.

Katherine and I went to Europe on our honeymoon, spending time mainly in Paris and Rome (where Katherine, who is a painter and currently working on a memoir of her youth living among the writers and artists of the New York School, was born). It was my first time in Europe and I was stunned. I remember being in the Luxemburg Gardens at twilight in November and I started to cry. It was so beautiful and I thought, here I am 24 years old, why have I had to wait until now to see this? I've been back to Europe several times, most recently to England, where Pablo Medina and I gave a reading tour from the Lorca book and our own books of poetry.

I've also spent a lot of time in Mexico, in Central America and South America. One of the most interesting times was my first time in Nicaragua, the largest country in the Central American Isthmus, bordered to the north by Honduras and Costa Rica to the south, This was in 1987/1988. It was during the time that the United States was waging a less than covert war against the Sandinista-led Nicaraguan government by funding the contras.

DA: Whatever compelled you to go to Nicaragua?

MS: I was down there as part of the Ruben Dario International Poetry Festival. Anne Waldman was there. Thomas McGrath was there. We felt like rock stars because we were taken around in buses, giving readings in stadiums, at the National Library. I was lucky in that I spoke Spanish and could sometimes go off on my own and wander around. It was amazing to me how many people knew poetry. I soon learned it was because poetry was a central part of the literacy program that had been instituted by Ernesto Cardenal and Mayra Jimenez. So everyone, from kids to older people to military, were learning to read and write by reading and writing poetry.

DA: You did find a spot teaching, which you actually enjoy.

MS: When we moved back to New York, to Brooklyn, in 1985, I started as a part-time faculty member at Eugene Lang College. I taught everything, journalism, creative writing, pedagogy. Eventually I became full-time and I'm currently an Associate Professor in Literary Studies.

I think teaching helps me as a poet, in a certain way, because I am constantly rereading and rethinking the poets I teach, and I am always trying to create new classes. The work is time consuming but I love to interact with students who are thinking poetry and literature. They are always giving me a fresh perspective on work I think I already know. I'm also fortunate to meet other writers and scholars who teach at Lang as well as other institutions. Lang has a particularly strong Literary Studies/Writing program. We have terrific faculty.

DA: Listener in the Snow: the Practice And Teaching of Poetry *has proven to be a valuable book*

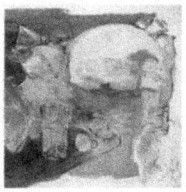

MS: I think what makes *Listener* an unusual book is that my plan was not to write a book about teaching; a book with lessons and student examples, though those do figure into the book. What interested me more was to write a collection of theme based inter-locking essays which included my poetry and fiction, the work of poets who have influenced me, and then show how those turned into lessons. I included a lot of the poems written by the students that came out of lessons. I think the key here is that I wanted it to be about the practice of poetry, how poetry happens. I didn't want it to be tricks or prompts but something deeper. I wanted it to show why poetry could be an exciting and integral part of anyone's life.

DA: You also co-edited an anthology, The Alphabet of the Trees: A Guide to Nature Writing.

MS: Yes, I did that with Christian McEwen. It came out in 2000, the same year as *Listener in the Snow* and was published by Teachers & Writers.

It has some wonderful contributors: Gary Snyder, Mary Oliver, Kim Stafford, to name some of the better known writers. Our idea then, as it remains now, was to provide readers with a chance to think about how to look at, think about, write, draw, experience nature in all possible ways. It is about the natural world in all ways, from the rural to the urban. The idea, in a sense, was, by exposing people to writing about nature, and providing some lessons, too, about how to be part of nature, people might begin to think of nature as something other than "the other." It seems to me, in this time when climate change is such an urgent issue, that this kind of work is more important now than ever.

DA: What are you working on now?

MS: I have several projects going. Because of my contract with Lavender Ink, next on the list is a new collection of poems, which I hope to have ready for 2015. I have also been working on a more long-term project, which is another translation, a substantial selection of poems of Mario Benedetti, Uruguayan journalist, novelist, and poet who was an integral member of the Generacion del 43.

My interest in Benedetti, who published more than 80 books and was published in 20 languages, as, I think, with my interest in Hinojosa, is that he is not well known, particularly for his poetry, in the English-speaking world. In the Spanish-speaking world he is considered one of Latin America's most important writers from the latter half of the 20th century.

Short term, I am also working on the poems of a young Uruguayan poet Martin Barrea Mattos. His work is profoundly good, though very difficult to translate since much of his poetry, which is both very serious and very funny, uses a lot of word play and puns, so he is forcing me to work in ways I haven't before. But that's one of the points of poetry, right? To think and work in ways one hasn't before.

Published in *Pif Magazine* February 1st, 2014

Poems by Mark Statman

a gift

from Jesse

no longer a baby
but just not
you held yourself up
by the kitchen window
backyards Brooklyn

you said
write me a poem
called a map of the winds

already you believed
there was something I could do

write me a poem

my happy sense
you believed I could
even if this one
wasn't mine to write

logos

tightening the stomach
of twisting overlay
of backhand doors
backward doors
trap doors
the opening closing
that becomes descent
or ascent
the world turned upside down
put into the box
any old box
this one came with
the grocery delivery
filled with vegetables
bottles, cans
box now taken out to the curb
recycle night
we put newspapers in
that's the urban
the rural
is the trip to the landfill
or dump
we called it a dump
as in what a dump
which is nowhere to live
though we've lived in some
our first Brooklyn apartment
got great light
we strung a hammock
from Mérida across
the big front room
a family hammock
double woven
threaded blue and pink
it sits now in a drawer

unused so many years
muffled street voices
muffled car sounds
what do you do
with these days
that stroll
from morning into afternoon
without interference
sometimes there is a hope
sometimes a prayer
what little music comes in
through the windows
is a fragment of
the music of the world
it was a car passing by
it was some people passing by
it was those clouds
or some kid
who jumped into
what was left on the street
of the puddles from
last night's rain
now the sun shines
for a second
the sun was in the puddle
but with that one jump
the puddle gone
that's the picture
right now
a puddle disappeared
by jump and sun
with words left over
to figure how to show
what was

William Trowbridge

William Trowbridge, whose most recent poetry collection, *Ship of Fool*, was published in 2011 by Red Hen Press, currently teaches in the University of Nebraska low-residency MFA in writing program. [Since this interview, Trowbridge has published his sixth poetry collection, *Put This On, Please: New and Selected Poems* (Red Hen Press, 2014).]He is also a Distinguished University Professor Emeritus at Northwest Missouri State, where he was co-editor of *The Laurel Review*, one of the Midwest's leading literary journals.

The other Trowbridge poetry collections are *Flickers* (2005), *O Paradise* (1995), and *Enter Dark Stranger* (1989), all from the University of Arkansas Press, as well as *The Complete Book Of Kong* (Southeast Missouri State University Press, 2003).

He is also the author of three poetry chapbooks, *The Packing House Cantata* (Camber Press, 2006), *The Four Seasons* (Red Dragonfly Press, 2001), and *The Book Of Kong* (Iowa State University Press, 1986). Trowbridge's poems have appeared in over 30 anthologies and textbooks, as well as in numerous literary journals, such as *The Gettysburg Review*, *The Georgia Review*, *Prairie Schooner*, *The Iowa Review*, and *New Letters*, to name a few.

Trowbridge earned a BA in Philosophy and an MA in English from the University of Missouri-Columbia, and went on to receive a Ph.D. in English from Vanderbilt University.

Trowbridge's awards include an Academy of American Poets Prize, a Bread Loaf Writers' Conference scholarship, a Pushcart Prize, and fellowships from The MacDowell Colony, Ragdale, The Anderson Center, and Yaddo. He was appointed Poet Laureate of Missouri in 2012 and will serve until April of 2015.

Trowbridge and his wife, Sue, live in Lee's Summit, MO.

Derek Alger: Congratulations on publication of your poetry collection Ship of Fool.

William Trowbridge: Thanks, Derek. It came out in February from Red Hen Press, whom I'm very happy to have as a publisher. The book centers around a character named Fool. When I first started writing poems about him, I wasn't quite sure who he was, other than an interesting character who seemed connected to the fool figure in silent films and stand-up comedy—for instance Buster Keaton, Laurel and Hardy, Richard Pryor, George Carlin. But when I got to know him better, I saw that he's connected to the fool archetype, which appears not only in silents and stand-ups but also in tales running back to the beginning of storytelling. To borrow from Yiddish comedy, he is a combination of  schlemiel and schlimazel. The difference, as you may know, is that the schlemiel is a bungler who's always accidentally breaking things and spilling stuff on people and the schlimazel is a sad sack who's always getting his things broken and getting stuff spilled on him. My Fool is both. He's often treated harshly, which seems to come simply from his being a fool. Most fool figures, though "comic," are subjected to a great deal of violence. The very term "slapstick" derives from this. In her book on the fool figure, Enid Welsford notes that the fool's essence is expressed in St. Chrysostom's phrase "he who gets slapped."

The fool's vulnerability and "foolishness" are seen by the non-fool population and perhaps by the fates as an invitation to take a shot—or at least be amused by watching someone or something else do so. The fool becomes a kind of scapegoat. Nathanael West, in *Day of the Locust*, discourses briefly but memorably on the fool or clown's tendency to incur violence—usually mirthful but sometimes not. People laugh when he gets slapped or slips on metaphorical or literal banana peels. Keaton discovered this as a child, when he was in his parents' vaudeville act. When their acrobatics began to feature little Buster taking what looked like, and often were, hard falls, the audience roared. The Keatons became a hit. I touch on the violence motivation fairly directly in several of the Fool poems. But, once in a while, the fool wins out, however temporarily and by default.

DA: Your fool is somewhat unique.

WT: My particular fool starts out as an angel who is accidentally cast into hell with Lucifer and company. He's then reincarnated in various historical times, with occasional unplanned visits back to the heavenly realm, run by an Enron-style-CEO God who rules from a kind of cosmic Corporate Woods. The first two sections of the book consist entirely of poems about Fool. The middle section is made up of sociopolitical and autobiographical poems, all of which touch on the idea of fools and foolishness.

DA: What prompted you to concentrate on a fool as a representative character of human existence, or is that a foolish question?

WT: Not foolish at all. Yes, I do see him as a reflection of an essential human trait, which is why this figure appears in all periods of literary history and, I'd guess, all cultures. I suppose we can consider our Edenic parents the first fools, and we've carried on the tradition without interruption ever since. It's in our blood. The fool represents human fallibility, and mine also represents the human capacity for hope in hopeless situations and a basic will towards goodness, however unreachable that may be in a world that is most often veering towards its opposite. Fool represents what the novelist Stanley Elkin called the main theme of modern comedy: powerlessness—specifically the powerlessness of the individual in the course of human history, especially modern history. So there's a seriousness beneath the comic surface in nearly all my Fool poems. This seriocomic element is present in the works of all my favorite writers and comedians. I think the tension created between comedy and seriousness generates an extra element of power in the works of authors who can maintain the risky balancing

DA: What was your childhood like?

WT: I'd say I had a pretty ordinary childhood in the Midwest, the home of ordinary childhoods. I was born in Chicago at the onset of WWII, and my father was called up by the Army to fight in Europe. So we moved around quite a bit during that time, from military base to military base, finally settling in Columbia, MO, my parents' hometown. When my father returned after VE Day, with a lingering case of PTSD (Post-traumatic stress disorder), we moved to Omaha, where he managed the Wilson & Co. packing house. Omaha had by then taken Chicago's title as "hog butcher for the world." Our house was devoid of art: no music, books, paintings. So my first exposure to art was when I watched the film classics run on early TV, when there wasn't much else offered in the way of programming. I was especially taken with the early comedians—Keaton, Laurel and Hardy, Chaplin, and later, Abbott and Costello—but the whole art form mesmerized me. The images still percolate through my subconscious and often turn up in my poems. From King Kong squashing pedestrians to Van Johnson cooking eggs in his helmet in *Battleground* to Jack Palance coldly gut-shooting Elisha Cook, Jr. in *Shane*, those images remain with me. When I was old enough to get to stay up late, my favorite time of the day became 10:30 p.m., when the late-night movie on TV started—a program known in Omaha as "Night Owl Theater." I remain a night owl. But at that time and all though high school, I had absolutely no interest in poetry and relatively little in any kind of reading.

DA: Did you have a specific idea of what you wanted to eventually do when you first went to college?

WT: My father, uncle, and big sister all graduated from the University of Missouri, and my grandfather had been Dean of Agriculture there. So I wound up there, too. I entered as a pre-med major, picturing myself as a future surgeon—about as realistic a notion as the old Walter Mitty pocketa, pocketa fantasy. I think about half the entering freshmen that year declared for pre-med. I found the pre-med courses both difficult and boring, so after my freshman year, I tried pre-law, a decision based on yet another fantasy. But even then, my main interest was in philosophy, which I finally switched to in hopes, I suppose, of becoming a professional wise person. I really did suspect that, with some help from the great thinkers, I could back Truth into a corner. Anyway, in college I became a reader. I was also taking a lot of lit courses then, which I discovered I enjoyed. It turned out that literature was something more than "Thanatopsis" and *The Good Earth*, the likes of which made up most of my high school literary curriculum. I planned to pursue a Ph.D. in philosophy, specializing in philosophical ideas in literature.

DA: So, Philosophy led you to English.

WT: Yes, that happened after I hit the Truth wall during my first semester of graduate studies in philosophy. Trying to slog my way though Aristotle's *Metaphysics* was perhaps the tipping point. Or maybe it was the required course in symbolic logic. Anyway, I finally realized my preference was definitely for the concrete particularity of literature over the abstractness of philosophy, though my interest in poetry was still minimal. I switched my major to literature, specifically modern American literature, with a planned specialty in Faulkner studies, and finished my MA at M.U.

DA: You took a break from academia.

WT: That's right. I went to Vanderbilt for my Ph.D., but after a semester there, I finally overdosed on school. I felt that, if I had to write one more essay test, I was going to have to do it under some kind of strong medication. I was granted a withdrawal in good standing from the program, which gave me the option of returning if my search for a life outside academia didn't pan out. I then undertook a series of interviews with newspapers, advertising agencies, publishers—anyone who might have a job for someone with an MA in English (I played down the philosophy degree). I was finally hired as a cub reporter for the *Des Moines Register and Tribune* in Iowa. I had absolutely no journalism experience, but I was lucky enough to walk in the door soon after the managing editor decided he was never going to hire another journalism major. He told me he wanted people who knew something beyond the history and principles of journalism and had not been trained to use a style different from the *Register and Tribune*'s. Ironically, he had turned down my journalist brother-in-law, Hugh Sidey, years before. Hugh went on to become White House correspondent for *Time* magazine. I wound up quitting the paper after a year.

DA: Sounds like it was time for a change.

WT: A job on the paper was the good news. The bad was that I learned I disliked journalism. I had visions of writing artsy features, not calling in police and fire stories from a closet-sized room in city hall. But I was being groomed for the latter. I had to compose the stories in my head, off my hastily scribbled notes, because the tight deadline left no time for me to sit down and write the stories. I dictated them to a "rewrite man," who typed out what I said and relayed it to an editor. So I couldn't see what I was writing till it came out in the paper—after it had been reshaped at the editorial desk. I also found that I had no interest in "getting the scoop" or getting in someone's face to pry information out of them. I realized I was a writer, not a reporter. So after a year of chasing scoops and getting rewritten, I gladly hurried back to Vanderbilt.

DA: It was at Vanderbilt you began to discover the poet within.

WT: That happened while I was studying for my Ph.D. comps. Modern poetry was one of the areas I would be tested over, so I was studying a lot of it. One day, after reading a poem by Howard Nemerov— "Mousemeal," as I recall—I found myself bitten by the poetry bug. I decided to try writing a poem, and after I did that, writing another. It felt so good that I wrote twelve or so during the next few weeks— before deciding to take them shyly to one of the professors to find out if they had any merit. He liked them enough to recommend that I enter the Academy of American Poets annual contest at Vanderbilt, and, to my utter surprise, I won. So that moment after I'd finished reading the Nemerov poem probably marked the beginning of my shift from scholarship to poetry, a shift that would take another five years or so to complete.

I left Vanderbilt ABD (all but dissertation) and took an assistant professorship at Northwest Missouri State. It required four years worth of summers to complete my Faulkner dissertation before I could concentrate on my poetry. After that, I began seriously shifting from scholarship to creative writing, though I'd spent my time as a student preparing to be a scholar. The only creative writing course I ever took was a fiction-writing course my sophomore year at M.U. So I now tell people who ask that I attended the Monkey-See-Monkey-Do School of Writing. I learned by imitating my favorite poets and then developing my own voice. There are both advantages and disadvantages to that compared to attending an MFA program in creative writing. You avoid the pressure that can develop to write for the small audience in your workshop, but you don't get regular feedback from your peers and instructors. I probably would have saved some development time by attending an MFA program, but by the time I realized that, it was too late to go back to school.

DA: We should probably mention your wife was a great support while you discovered and followed your true calling.

WT: Yes, she certainly was. We had dated some in Omaha in high school, but her family moved to Minnesota her senior year and we wound up going to different universities. But we got back together our senior year and were married right after college. She'd earned an education degree from the University of Minnesota, and she took a job in special education while I worked on my master's degree at M.U. As you might guess, special ed. is a high-stress-low-reward field, requiring a lot of dedication and inner strength. From the beginning of our marriage, she was very supportive of my meandering toward becoming a poet. We had our first child when I was working on my MA and wound up with three after I'd been teaching full-time for a while. She bore the larger share of child rearing while I was in school and after that as well. Her last job before retirement was as a language arts teacher in Maryville, MO, middle school, where Northwest Missouri State is located. She now does volunteer work and enjoys, as I do, visiting our kids and grandkids.

DA: And then you pursued the balancing act of teaching and writing poetry.

WT: That's right. I was hired as an American lit scholar at Northwest and didn't get to teach a creative writing course till I'd published enough poems to make my case for doing so. However, the school had only two creative writing courses, one in poetry and one in fiction. I mainly taught graduate courses in the novel, plus some survey courses and freshman English. There was a 14-hour per semester course load there, which didn't leave a lot of time for writing. Teaching is a very demanding job if you take it seriously, and I did. So, yes, I had to do a balancing act between the writing and teaching, and teaching took up most of my time during the school year. I know that some say that teaching energizes their writing, but I think that doing it well can have the opposite effect. It did for me. I wound up getting most of my writing done during holidays and in the summer. I stopped teaching in the summer after one or two times to get more writing time.

DA: You also discovered the value of writing retreats and fellowships.

WT: Retreats were precious to me. Yaddo was my first and is still my favorite. I was accepted for a month there, but before arriving, I began to worry that I'd freeze up and sit around watching squirrels for a month. I didn't realize the energizing effect of having your time protected for the sole purpose of writing. I went to Yaddo for a month and, right afterwards, to The MacDowell Colony for another month, and had almost a year's worth of work finished when I came home. And, of course, I got to bask in the literary history of those two venerable retreats, not to mention hanging around with a lot of interesting people in the evening. I've also been to Ragdale and The Anderson Center, with much the same results. And, though Bread Loaf is not a retreat in the sense of getting writing done, it was my first exposure to the rubbing of shoulders with a lot of writers. I was pretty starry-eyed. That was where I got to meet Howard Nemerov for the first time. I went there as a working scholar in 1981, and I'm still in contact with several people I met there.

DA: How did your collection The Complete Book Of Kong Poems *come about?*

WT: I wrote my first Kong poem, "Kong Looks Back on His Tryout with the Bears," with no intention of writing any more. But that poem gave me an idea for another and the next yet another. Motivated partly by my attraction to the old 1933 version of the film and partly by a sense that Kong embodies something very human, I wound up with 25 or 30 pages of Kong poems. X.J. Kennedy, in an essay called "Who Killed King Kong?" persuasively argues that Kong is an example of the pitiable monster archetype, a figure who's good or at least well-meaning inside but is trapped in a monstrous body, which hides that goodness from the world. I found in Kong yet another figure in which to combine seriousness with comedy. Like Quasimodo, the Frankenstein monster, the beast in *Beauty and the Beast*, that monster must suffer and eventually die alienated from fellow creatures. Once again, this figure becomes an archetype because he reflects something in us, who sometimes feel the world doesn't see the beautiful person deep inside our unbeautiful exterior. Kong may be a monster, but he is as vulnerable and lonely as any of his human counterparts. I didn't make the Kong poems into a book till about 15 years after I'd written the original poems. It somehow took that long to make me realize that, if I wrote 15 or 20 more, I'd have a book.

DA: We should mention you gained valuable experience with a well-respected literary journal.

WT: Some NWMSU colleagues and I rescued *The Laurel Review* from West Virginia Wesleyan College in 1986. I had been reading fiction for them for a couple of years when the editor, Mark DeFoe, told me he was going to let it die. He'd been editing it by himself for years and was exhausted. It took us a couple of years to get subscriptions back up, but after NWMSU gave each of us a one-class teaching-load reduction, we managed to turn it into a very respectable literary magazine. We published well-known writers like William Stafford and Albert Goldbarth, but we also managed to get many new writers into print. It was very time-consuming work, but we were passionate about it. We prided ourselves on producing handsome, error-free issues containing some of the best writing in America. I got to know a lot more other writers during my editorship and am still in contact with many of them. I left the magazine when I took early retirement in 1998, but it's still going.

DA: You still keep your hand in teaching.

WT: Yes, I teach part-time in the University of Nebraska Low-residency MFA in Writing Program. I got in on it at the beginning and continue to teach there. At first, I was a little worried about getting involved, because of its extensive use of the internet in place of regular classes, but I was quickly won over. The program caught fire the first semester and has continued that way ever since. The students are bright, enthusiastic, and hard-working. The faculty, too, is first rate. The learning is intense, with an emphasis on one-to-one student-faculty relationships. The faculty are called "mentors" instead of professors, and we're restricted to a maximum of five students a semester. That allows students much more personal attention and flexibility than conventional programs do. I mentor two students a semester. And the residency part is held in a resort hotel in Nebraska City rather than on the Lincoln campus. So students and faculty have their own hotel rooms instead of dorm rooms and eat in the restaurant instead of in a cafeteria. And the part-time load leaves me plenty of time for my own literary endeavors. I plan to keep teaching there till I can't tell metaphors from Metamucil, though they may ask me to retire before that.

Published in *Pif Magazine* June 3rd, 2011

Poems by William Trowbridge

BASIC FOOL

"Get down and give me twenty!"
snaps Cupid. Fool pumps away,
boots burnished, seams crisp,
making choo-choo sounds.
"Show me your love face,
snarls the cherub after Fool
wobbles to attention. "LOVE
FACE, maggot!" Cupid shrieks
as Fool mugs like a chimpanzee
having a stroke. Fool starts
to think he should have tried
something easier, like
fire eating or celibacy.
After a night of introspection,
he hijacks a tank and drives
over Cupid, leaving a trail
of feathers and baby fat.
Later, he takes a high-speed
joyride in somebody's Porsche

with a waitress he's picked up.
"You may not believe this,"
Fool tells her right before
the blowout, "but I'm a flyboy
from the infantry of love."

FOOL'S PARADISE

Fool, who was standing too close when God
swept the rebel seraphim into perdition, tries,
as the former Lucifer exhorts, to make a heaven
of Hell. After all, feeling your eyeballs boil inside
keeps your mind off your smoldering testicles.
And there's practically no dress code, other than
that coat of film you get from the burning
bodily discharges. "This is great," he tells himself,
scalp bubbling. "Good as Heaven. Better."

He trades the key to his Heavenly treasure
to Moloch for a lighter pitchfork and membership
in the Gehenna Debating Society. He joins
the Woeful Chamber of Commerce, where he initiates
Bingo Night. When the morale of the damned rises
56 percent, he gives off-shore real estate a try.

But the now-Satan thinks he smells a power play,
and God's wrath rattles the cosmic chandelier
when half the cherubim start flying weekends
to some new spot called the Lake of Fire
Floating Oasis. The two hold secret talks
in a neutral galaxy, where, after a thousand years,
they negotiate a win-win solution.

Fool finds himself near the La Brea Tar Pits,
in the first of his innumerable earthly lives,
and Satan gets to use a gigantic flaming sword

to chase Adam and Eve out of Eden to a world
where they and their baffled descendants
are subject to sin, disease, insanity, and death,
all of which are invented for this occasion.
Fool takes a deep breath of miasma, feels groggy.
"This is great," he declares. "Couldn't *be* better."

Pamela Uschuk

Political activist and wilderness advocate, Pam Uschuk has howled out six books of poems, including *Crazy Love*, winner of a 2010 American Book Award, *Finding Peaches in the Desert* (Tucson/PimaLiteraature Award), and *Wild in the Plaza of Memory* (2012). A new collection of poems, *Blood Flower*, was published in January 2015.

Translated into more than a dozen languages, her work appears in over three hundred journals and anthologies worldwide, including *Poetry, Ploughshares, Agni Review, Parnassus Review*, etc.

Uschuk has been awarded the 2011 War Poetry Prize from Winning 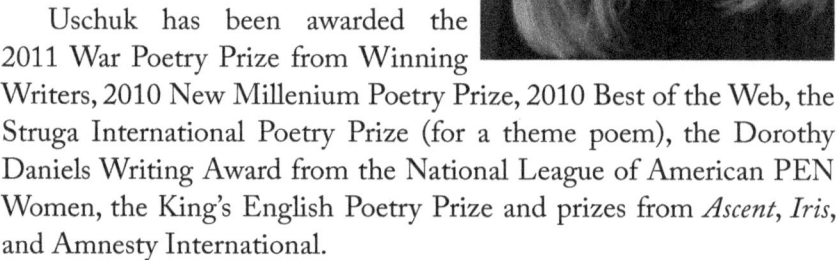 Writers, 2010 New Millenium Poetry Prize, 2010 Best of the Web, the Struga International Poetry Prize (for a theme poem), the Dorothy Daniels Writing Award from the National League of American PEN Women, the King's English Poetry Prize and prizes from *Ascent, Iris*, and Amnesty International.

Associate Professor of Creative Writing at Fort Lewis College and Editor-In-Chief of *Cutthroat, A Journal of the Arts*, Uschuk lives in Bayfield, Colorado. She also has a home in Tucson, Arizona. Uschuk is often a featured writer at the Prague Summer Programs and was the 2011 John C. Hodges Visiting Writer at University of Tennessee, Knoxville. She's working on a multi-genre book called *The Book of Healers Healing; An Odyssey Through Ovarian Cancer*.

> "Like Lorca, Uschuk is a poet of the duende, that mystical Spanish conception; she views the poem as a vehicle for fierce engagement with the body and its social realities, often with a metaphysical awareness that transcends and extends

the corporeal into the natural world. Working a poetics rare for a North American writer, Uschuk has crafted a poetry equally steeped in nature and political resistance. This is an ecological poetics of engagement, a mythic poetry—part Lorca, part Rachel Carson."

—Sean Thomas Dougherty, *Rain Taxi*, 2012

Derek Alger: Let's start at the beginning. Where were you born and raised?

Pamela (Marie) Uschuk: I was born in Lansing, Michigan on the hottest day of the year, my mother delighted in telling me. She said that mine was an easy birth. I grew up on an 80-acre working farm 7 miles from the village of DeWitt and 12 miles from Lansing, close enough for my Dad to drive to the Oldsmobile factory to work. The farm was lush, green and beautiful, our yard studded with leafy maples and elms, a hickory tree and flower gardens where roses, Canturbury bells, snap dragons, sweet Williams, lilacs, tiger lilies and more flourished, all tended by my mother. She was an excellent gardener. We raised black angus cattle, chickens, pigs, wheat, corn, oats and we grew a gigantic vegetable garden. Even though we were poor, we always had plenty of good food to eat, what they would call organic now.

DA: Food for thought is always good.

PMU: As I grew older, I felt increasingly isolated on the farm. Because I wasn't allowed to have a car, I was stuck there. Having a mother who was severely bi-polar compounded my agony. She was hospitalized in psychiatric wards every couple of years for paranoia and wild, but not fun for us, hallucinations. She underwent electric shock treatments and psychotherapy. There was no real cure. In those barbaric psychiatric days, the drug of choice was thorazine, which made her a zombie. My mother was very smart, sensitive, an avid reader and she played the piano and organ, but her delusions immobilized her and terrified us.

And, she could also be manipulative, deftly playing the martyr. The older I grew, the less I was able to communicate with her. When my mother was ill, I, being oldest, had to take care of my brother and sisters while my father was at work. Her disorder affected and traumatized our entire lives. Our family spun on the tilt-a-whirl of her frequent psychotic episodes.

Ironically, after my father's death, I ended up being the prime caretaker for my mother for much of the last five years of her life. My anger and resentment slowly turned to compassion for her, for her terrorizing delusions, her isolation, loneliness, and the box canyon of sadness she couldn't escape. Almost too late, I learned to love my mother. Sometimes taking care of her constant needs felt like an imposition, but I've come to understand that it was also a huge gift I'm still unwrapping. I've written about her in poetry and prose, and I continue to untangle the web of my knotty childhood.

DA: You also have a deep love for animals.

PMU: As for my relationship with animals, I had and have today a deep respect for and love of animals. I've always had pets. They've saved my sanity, if not my life. Animals, both domestic and wild, are trustworthy and are mainly without guile. A lot can be learned about the behavior of people by studying the behavior of animals. My childhood companions were rabbits, white tail deer, foxes, raccoons, oppossums, skunks, frogs, snakes, snapping and painted turtles and toads. As a child, I loved roaming our farm with my brother, John. We had free run of our eighty acres and the ponds nearby. As over-protective as my father was at times, it was astonishing how much latitude he allowed us in terms of mobility on the farm and in its local environs. This was liberating and made us self-sufficient. We had to rely on our imaginations to invent games to amuse ourselves. Out of necessity, we became acute observers of the natural world. We lived it.

There is no doubt that being such an intimate part of and enjoying so deeply the natural world fired a life-long passion for wilderness and its inhabitants.

DA: Your father was quite an influence on you.

PMU: My father was a large man, the son of a Russian immigrant who was also a gangster. My grandfather was a member of the Purple Gang and was sent to prison for murder. He was a member of the aristocracy in Byelorussia, but his family forced him, because of his bad behavior, to leave home and to emigrate to America. My father bore the brunt of my grandfather's wrath and so reacted against him. Early on, my father instilled in us the importance of telling the truth and obeying the law.

When my grandfather committed suicide, my father had to drop out of the 10th grade to go to work to help my grandmother support the family. He was a decorated hero in World War II in the Army Air Corps, a tail gunner who fought in Northern Africa and Italy, then re-enlisted and was sent to the South Pacific. In Australia, he went AWOL and hopped trains all around the country. He was especially fascinated by the Aborigines. Because the Air Corps lost his paperwork, my father spent two years on New Guinea in the jungle, where he started a jewelry business and where he survived typhoid fever, among other things. He had a lifelong interest in Indigenous peoples. As a child, I loved hearing about his adventures, which included my father and a pilot friend of his hijacking a shipment of Johnny Walker Scotch meant for MacArthur's headquarters. They passed the bottles of scotch out to every soldier they saw in Port Moresby. My father was busted for that, but he said it was worth it. My mother disapproved of his telling those stories. My brother, sisters and I begged to hear more.

To say that my father had a profound effect on me is understating it. I was terrified of his temper. He could yell louder than anyone I knew, but he also actively played with us. He was fun. He drew pictures with us. He took us to movies, he hiked with us, picked berries with us, played football and baseball with us, and drove us to Lake Michigan for all-day family outings at the beach. We did everything as a family, complete with cousins, aunts, uncles and my grandma & step-grandpa. My father taught us to love the woods, taught us not to kill anything simply for sport, and he taught us to fight injustice. At the Oldsmobile factory, my father was a Union Steward so he wasn't popular with the bosses. One of his crusades was fighting for the right of black women to use the bathroom at the Oldsmobile Plant. One thing he absolutely insisted upon was that his children get a good education. After all, his education had been rudely curtailed. He was a reader—he consumed two newspapers a day, and he read history books. My father was complex so it's difficult to pigeon-hole him in this small space. He had a great and deep laugh, was as warm and loving as he was spiteful and intolerant of stupidity. It was hard to gauge when he'd explode into inexplicable anger, which made life very tricky for us. Extremely quick-witted, he often used his wit to denigrate his enemies and, unfortunately, us kids and my mother.

When I was three, my father had me memorize the entire poem, "The Night Before Christmas," which I recited without a glitch in front of relatives at Christmas. Some of my earliest memories are of me sitting on his lap while he read the newspaper to me. He taught me to read very early. As a child, I loved rhythms, loved words. I remember carrying around a small tablet to write words and their meanings on—I was fascinated by them. I read books as if they were food, and the dictionary became one of my favorite volumes. Because I was so isolated in high school, I read 5th Century Greek plays, Shakespeare, all of Saul Bellow, J.D. Salinger, Kurt Vonnegut, etc.

My life was further complicated because our household was multi-lingual. My father and his siblings were fluent in Russian. My beloved grandmother, Anna, and my step-grandfather spoke Russian and Czech in their home. Their friends spoke Polish, Armenian, Rumanian, Bulgarian and other Slavic tongues. The music and rich textures of these languages resonate in my poems today.

DA: Where did you go to college?

PMU: I earned a BA in English from Central Michigan University. My high school grades and my SAT scores were high so I received a four year scholarship that paid all the tuition and fees to attend CMU. I could have gone to any school in Michigan, like the University of Michigan.

Maybe I should have. I was scared that the U of M was too big. After all, I was a farm girl and had attended a very small high school. I chose CMU because my cousin went there. In college, I was very poor and ate a lot of macaroni & cheese and Ramen because they were cheap.

As an undergraduate, I was an art major for my first two years, but I was frustrated by the ambiguity of the art professors. They didn't know how to explain technique. Their vague, "You know, just do it," left me befuddled. My childhood dream was somewhere between Paul Gaughin and Mahatma Ghandi—I wanted to be a great artist and to change the world. I decided that if I wasn't going to be a great painter, I'd be a great writer.

I adored literature classes, especially because I loved to read. In literature classes, we discussed books critically. That was a treat. I was propagandized by my family into becoming a public school teacher. It was a safe profession for women. Since I admired some of my teachers, I thought that it could be a career that would fulfill me.

During high school, I was placed in accelerated writing courses because of my writing ability, so I thought an English degree would be a good fit. Those accelerated writing classes and my science classes kept high school from being a total bore. After graduating with honors from CMU, I received a full graduate teaching fellowship to study Comparative Literature with a concentration in Russian Literature. Although, I loved my classes, I was restless. One year into an unhappy marriage, I felt like my life was belted into a straight jacket. I needed something, but I wasn't sure what. Then it struck me. I'd been in school most of my life. I moved to the woods outside of Traverse City to learn the names and habits of the birds, the animals, plants and trees. I needed survival skills I couldn't get in academia.

DA: But you did end up teaching.

PMU: Yes, I did. After substitute teaching for a bit, I signed a contract for my first teaching job at Elk Rapids Middle School. Like every public school teacher, I was overworked and underpaid. I taught six classes a day, everything from English to Oceanography (because they had no one else to teach it!). I was a very popular teacher and worked not only with regular students but with juvenile offenders that were sent up from Detroit to get them out of their bad environments. They brought crime to our community. I remember one 6th grader, a cute little blonde who brought me a photo of her teenaged brother dead in a casket. She'd taken the photo. Her brother had been shot to death by police. Anyway, although I loved my students, I was exhausted. I'd plop down in front of the TV every night after school and turn into a turnip. I wanted simply to write, so I quit my teaching job mid-year during my fourth year. My students protested and marched around the school with big signs, trying to get me to come back. It was touching. As much as I was flattered, I was adamant. Following Rilke's admonishment, I looked to "change my life." For the next two months, I wrote 16 hours a day and finished a 365 page novel I called *Flip Side Memorial*. I revised it twice, then put it into a shoe box. It was my breakaway work.

DA: And where's the novel now?

PMU: Still in the witness protection program, living under an assumed name in the shoebox.

DA: I walked into that one.

PMU: While I was working on the novel, I continued to write poems. I just didn't feel they were good enough for public consumption. They weren't, but my illusions kept me writing poem after poem. The novel compelled me, but I couldn't give up the poetry. She was the seductress that won my heart.

DA: A change of career really convinced you that you were meant to write poetry.

PMU: There was nothing else that made me as happy, as ecstatic, as excited or as miserable as writing poetry. Of all genres, for me, poetry is the most difficult thing to write. As corny as this sounds and is, writing poems gave my life depth and meaning. My poetry came out of my best self, not the self that whined and blundered through life. Writing was power. It was a way for me to smash the walls of my small existence, to find my way out of my own head and to fly along this journey.

DA: You ran into some major influences along the way.

PMU: When I moved to Northern Michigan, I met Jim Harrison, who my next husband, Jerry Gates, knew and we ended up hanging out with him and the Lelanau County version of the Merry Pranksters. Through Harrison, I once met Thomas McGuane, who was the most handsome man I'd ever seen. I liked his smile and his stories. Harrison was a smart ass, cynical, glitzy with a gritty, rebellious sort of fame. In the Hemingway macho tradition, he flirted outrageously with me as he did every other young attractive woman. We drank and played pool and partied too much in Dick's Bar. I was young and enscorseled with Harrison's wit and humor, and mightily admired the multiple intelligences, the pathos in his poetry. I read everything he wrote, and I wanted to write as well as he did. No, I wanted to write better than he did.

DA: Another poet had a profound influence on you.

PMU: Yes, there were many actually—Theodore Roethke, Richard Braughtigan, Sylvia Plath were some of my models. It was Galway Kinnell who actually took an interest in my poetry. After quitting my teaching job, I became a bartender and I wrote a lot of poems during that time. I attended all the poetry readings I could—Joseph Brodsky, Philip Levine, Diane Wakoski, Gary Snyder, Marvin Bell, Harrison. When Galway Kinnell came to Interlochen Arts Academy to read, my life changed. I was mesmerized by his poems and the way he read them as if he were standing in a cathedral reciting secret texts. Somehow I got invited to a private after-reading party for him. We talked intensely. Galway invited me and my friend, Mike Masley, to sit in on his poetry workshop at Cranbrook Institute. Mike, my sister Judi, and I drove downstate for that. Kinnell's workshop was great, and he asked me to send him more poems. Among others, I sent "Waiting for Nighthawk in a Snowstorm" and "Elk Camp." Kinnell wrote back that my poems were intelligent, the imagery fresh and vital and that I should keep writing. Those were words I needed to hear.

DA: And then you were fortunate to find a great husband and poet in one.

PMU: When William Pitt Root came to Interlochen as Visiting Poet, I had given up on men and relationships. My second marriage had long been in shambles. None of my lovers worked out. Although I was still bartending, I was teaching occasional writing workshops for Pathfinder, a private school, and I was traveling back and forth across the country alone. I was running a small monthly reading series in Traverse City with a tiny bit of money from the Michigan Council on the Arts. Anyway, Bill came to Interlochen, and I wanted him to read in my series. I was also commissioned to write an article on him for the Traverse City Record Eagle. When I called Bill and asked him to read, he asked me how much I could pay. I told him, "$50." He said, "That isn't enough, but would you like to go to a movie." Needless to say, this caught me totally off-guard. I also laughed, "Okay, I'll go to a movie with you if I can bring some of my friends." I asked him how I'd recognize him. He said he'd be wearing a Panama drifter. I told him I would wear a black rose.

    I brought 12 of my friends with me to the theatre. We saw "A Little Romance." After the movie, my friends abandoned us, so I took Bill to a colorful local Traverse City bar to play pool and have a beer. We had more fun than I imagined and we couldn't stop talking. We became friends. I read Bill's work, loved it, and then I did my interview with him. We shared poems. He did read in my reading series without charging a thing. It wasn't until the next month that we became more than friends. I found my muse in Bill, who shared, with equal intensity, my love of dogs, thrift stores, chocolate, wilderness and a gypsy appetite for adventure. When I moved from Michigan to Oklahoma City to live with Bill, my life broke open like a ripe plum. We've been lovers and friends ever since.

    When Bill left Northern Michigan for Oklahoma City, it wasn't long before I decided to leave also. I headed for Colorado. While living there with my brother, Bill invited me to visit him in Oklahoma, which I did. The rest is history, as they say. Fate wouldn't allow us to stay away from one another. A month later, we moved in together. During those first three years, we lived in Oklahoma City, Port Townsend, Washington, Missoula, Montana, Oracle, Arizona, then back to Missoula, where Bill was hired to replace Richard Hugo after Hugo passed away.

DA: You received your MFA in Fiction and in Poetry from the University of Montana.

PMU: I received my MFA in 1986. While I was a graduate student, I was also a Poet In Schools.

    I volunteered to work on Indian reservations, and ended up working for three years with students from the Assiniboine, Sioux, Salish, Flathead, Blackfeet, Northern Cheyenne, Nez Perce and Crow tribes. It was a tough job because I had to drive so far for my week-long residencies. I stayed in cheap motels, where I created poetry lessons and I wrote many poems myself. I was also Editor-In-Chief of *Cutbank*, the literary magazine out of the University of Montana. One of the wonderful things about attending the U of M was the exposure to and close contact with well-known writers that graduate students had. So many writers, editors and agents came through Missoula—that was great. During graduate school, I had short-term workshops from Donald Hall, Denis Johnson, T.C. Boyle, Leslie Silko, Stephanie Vaughn, Tobias Wolff, among others, and I studied with Patricia Goedicke, William Kitteridge, Bill and Joy Harjo, who held the First Richard Hugo Chair in Poetry. Bill and Joy were two of the most influential and best poetry teachers I ever had.

DA: Your teaching experience can be described as one with extensive variety and many geographical stops.

PMU: I'll try to condense this. My husband took a position teaching creative writing at Hunter College in Manhattan, so in fall 1986, we moved to New Paltz, New York. I applied for several entry level positions and took an adjunct job at Marist College across the Hudson River in Poughkeepsie. I volunteered to teach composition in their prison program, thinking that it would be a worthwhile experience, that prisons like reservations are places where I might effect the most positive change and make a difference, a sort of a giving back to society. I've always believed that I need to be socially responsible, to do what good I can in the world.

That adjunct job last six years, and was one of the most intense teaching experiences of my life. I taught in Greenhaven, a maximum security prison for men in upstate New York. Half my students were convicted murderers. A Puerto Rican woman gave me good advice the first night I went to teach there. She told me to never show fear. I remembered that. It served me well, even when I was threatened by an inmate who ended up in the psyche ward.

I got a good reputation, teaching poetry and short fiction. I built the Creative Writing program in that prison. John Cheever had taught Creative Writing there, where he set his novel, *Falconer*.

I had a legacy to uphold, but teaching in prison erodes the soul in many ways. I lasted six years, and I am proud of what I did there. My students were serious writers, and they wrote amazing pieces, some of which found their way into print. They felt safe in my workshop. Those students ranged from an ex-Black Panther to an Afghani diamond smuggler to an Israeli mercenary soldier who was fluent in five languages to criminals in prison for drug-related crimes. It was interesting, but I could never let down my guard. Speaking of guards, the guards resented us and the program. The inmates were getting educations the majority of these guards had no access to or intelligence for. My supervisor was a chauvinist plus. After six years, I said goodbye.

DA: This interview is more about you than your poetry, so I'll just recommend readers buy your work, but we should touch on it a bit.

PMU: My poems usually begin in the natural world, somehow, or with natural imagery, but then they expand outward and encompass things like politics, wilderness preservation, preservation of the wild within us, compelling stories of people fighting for justice, the interconnectedness of everything in the universe, human relationships, land, spirituality, etc. It's important to me to write about what moves me so I have often told the stories of those people or creatures who have no voice or whose voices have been suppressed in some way.

Exposing injustice for the evil it is is utterly important to me. There is so much corruption, hatred, greed, brutality and mistrust in the world, that it is utterly important for poetry to hold out truth, to hold out compassion, to hold out light and especially love to all of us.

In this way, it is a balance or songs of balance. As Joy Harjo said so brilliantly, "We must turn slaughter into food." The past eight years, I've been consumed with injustices arising from our own government's corruption and it's many abuses of power. The Bush administration has been a disaster for families, for health care, for the environment, for the economy, for every day Americans, and I've written a lot about that.

The Iraq War was an invasion conducted on misformation, at best, lies, at worst. It has nearly bankrupted us as a nation, created enemies for us all over the globe, not to mention caused the deaths and maimings of hundreds of thousands of soldiers and civilians. All these things happen to real people and are grounded in real stories. They are not just a matter of statistics or political maneuvering. As a poet, I don't think I have any choice but to address these issues.

DA: That's quite a compliment that your collection, Finding Peaches in the Desert, *was made into a CD of the same name with musical accompaniment by Chameleon and Joy Harjo.*

PMU: As I mentioned, I met Joy in 1985 at the University of Montana when she held the first Richard Hugo Chair. I took a graduate poetry workshop with her. Joy was a unique and remarkable teacher, the best teacher of poetry, beside Bill, that I've ever had. She and I became very close friends and remain so today. We believe in each other's work and in each other.

DA: Shifting back to your childhood, your grandmother was also a great influence.

PMU: No, she was central, an axis that kept me from flying off into the abyss. My Grandma, Anna, was the only adult who did not judge me. She let me be me, laughed with me, walked in the woods with me, picked wild strawberries, raspberries, plums and wildflowers with me, took me to movies, and rocked me in her front porch swing while telling me stories about her life.

I spent a lot of time with my grandmother, who I absolutely adored. She was a strong woman, independent, smart and with a razor-edged sense of humor. Although she stood at 4'10", she never seemed small. Everyone, even my giant father, deferred to her.

My grandmother came to this country in that great turn of the 19th Century wave of Eastern European immigrants. She was only 16, and she spoke no English. When her two brothers, then her brewery owning father died, it sent the remains of her family into chaos. My great-grandmother believed in streets paved with gold, so she took a chunk of money and sent it to a cousin in New York, who was supposed to take that money to set up my grandmother. When my grandmother arrived on a boat from Czechloslovakia, that weasel cousin sold her to a sweat shop in Philadelphia. She rolled cigars 16 hours a day, six days a week, until she ran away with a circus.

Yes, my grandma sang and danced in the circus, and I wish I could have seen her. My grandfather saw her perform in the circus and fell in love with her. When my grandfather committed suicide in the 30s, my grandmother took in laundry and worked as a maid in Lansing to keep the state from taking away her children. She was a fierce defender of her family. My grandmother remains one of my most powerful role models.

DA: It must have been very special being a featured writer at Prague Summer Workshops.

PMU: It was and is a great honor. I have Richard Katrovas, the dynamic and wonderful Director of the program, to thank for that. The program brings in top-notch writers of fiction, poetry, nonfiction and playwriting to work with highly-motivated, accomplished graduate and undergraduate students from the U.S. and Europe. It is a joy to participate in this program.

There is also the draw of my Czech heritage. To walk the same cobblestones as my grandmother reconnects me with her indomitable spirit. I hear her speak in every shop and restaurant I enter. The elegant architecture, the beautiful bridges, the proliferation of culture, the Pinkus Synagogue, the Jewish Cemetery, Kafka's old haunts, the Terezin Concentration Camp, the Communist Museum, the square where Jan Palka incinerated himself in protest of the Russian occupation of Czechloslovakia, all have a profound effect on me. I've been an Honored Guest twice at the Prague Summer Workshops, and I am grateful to be teaching poetry there in July 2009.

DA: Tell the truth, did you ever picture yourself one day standing 12,000 feet in the Himalayas of Tibet with a group students and your husband?

PMU: No, I didn't picture myself standing with students in the Himalayas, but I long dreamed of going there. I can see the way that path evolved.

When I was a senior in high school, I began reading about and studying Buddhism. I read and was affected by the novel, *Siddhartha*. Tibetan Buddhism still holds a great amount of wisdom and appeal for me. I took students to Northern India, to Ladahk (Little Tibet) to study Buddhist sacred scripture, art and culture. We climbed to monasteries at dizzying heights, met with monks and shaman and common Tibetan people who had the most amazing serenity and happiness. Going to Dharamsala and twice seeing the Dalai Lama was astonishing and changed me in unending ways. I've written some long poems from that experience, as well as two articles that appeared last year in *Parabola* and in T*errain Magazine*. I will be digesting that trip, those experiences for the rest of my life. That I could share them with my husband is an incredible blessing. I am a traveler, by nature, and so is my husband, and I hope that we can continue to see and explore and learn the world together.

So far, we've been to nearly every state in the U.S., to many countries in Europe and Eastern Europe, all over Mexico, to Hawaii, in South Africa, India and the Himalayas together. We are very lucky.

DA: You can be found these days, among other things, teaching creative writing at Fort Lewis College in Durango, Colorado.

PMU: Yes, I have a Creative Writing tenure-track teaching position. This semester, I teach a beginning poetry workshop, a senior poetry workshop, and a screenwriting class. My students are intellectually curious, enthusiastic and many are as obsessed with writing as I am.

Fort Lewis College is located at 7000 feet on top of a mesa that overlooks Durango, the entire La Plata Range of the Rockies and the Animas River valley. Physically, this is one of most breathtaking campuses I've ever walked. The college is a four-year undergraduate liberal arts institution. The students are independent-minded, resourceful, tough and are here, for the most part, because they love the mountains and the natural world. On the downside, when it snows and there is new powder in the mountains, students skip classes en masse to hit the slopes with snowboards and skiis. Because Fort Lewis is the only four-year college in the United States where Native American students attend without paying tuition, we have a high Native American enrollment—125 tribes are represented. There are also Caucasian, Hispanic, and African American students, plus foreign exchange students from various places on the globe. I love this kind of rich cultural diversity in the classes and at public school functions. A Ute Medicine man often gives a blessing at such affairs as Convocation and Graduation. Walking across campus, I can stop to buy fry bread, then indulged in a green chili burro on my way to class. If I'm lucky, I'll catch a glimpse of our resident mountain lion.

DA: And finally tell us a bit about Cutthroat *and how it came into being.*

PMU: That's another big question with a long answer, but I'll try not to enter a wind tunnel. When I was a graduate student at the

University of Montana, I was Editor-In-Chief of its literary magazine, *Cutbank*. Although this job was time-consuming and entailed big-time responsibility, including fund-raising, I liked reading other writers' work and publishing good stories and poems. I was fascinated with the process. Being a bit OCD, editing, with its endless details work, called me.

After grad school, I harbored a dream to publish a magazine. My husband, Bill, had plenty of experience editing, too. He and Gurney Norman started the *Penny Papers* in California, and that was a great success. We both thought it would be as much fun as a mare's nest to run our own magazine. So, when Bill took early retirement from his teaching job at Hunter College, and I quit my teaching job at Salem College in North Carolina, we moved to Colorado and plunged in the literary river. We had no funding, but we did have a credit card. We came up with the name *Cutthroat: A Journal of the Arts* after Colorado's beautiful endangered trout. Since we know a fair amount of writers, we solicited work from some friends and enlisted others to be our Contributing Editors. We took out ads in *Poets & Writers* and *AWP Chronicle*, and we began receiving submissions for our first issue. To date, we've published work by Marvin Bell, Joy Harjo, Michael Blumenthal, Richard Jackson, Fred Chappell, Kelly Cherry, Rebecca Seiferle, Michael Waters, Cynthia Hogue, Rick DeMarinis, Linda Hogan, Wendell Berry, Dorianne Laux, Alfred Corn, and TR Hummer and many other fine writers. And, we've published many unknown and talented writers.

I instituted national writing competitions at both *Cutbank* and the Salem College Center for Women Writers (I directed that Center from 2002-2005), and so we ran our first contests, naming them the Joy Harjo Poetry Contest and the Rick DeMarinis Short Fiction Contest. These continue to be very popular contests, and our magazine's reputation keeps growing, so far without groaning. In our forthcoming issue, we are publishing a story by a writer from Kazakhstan, poems by a Maori poet, by an Australian poet, a story by a Japanese-American as well as new poems from Elise Paschen, Wendell Berry, Linda Hogan, Richard Jackson, Dennis Sampson, and a new story by Karen Brennan. No matter this bad economy, we intend to keep *Cutthroat* alive.

Published in *Pif Magazine* March 13th, 2009

Poems by Pamela Uschuk

A SIBERIAN COLD FRONT TAKES OVER THE LAST WEEK OF APRIL

Siberia, I do not need your sleet today,
impaling me like a fork in a cheek.
Not that you don't feel free to crowd my life with ancestors,
memories of bear paws and shrill white distances
cracking the civilized seams of my brain.
Today, Siberia, my head aches with your steel humidity,
cold as a slug's mucous skirts,
slick as the stone pipe of a shamanka.
I'd like to refuse your telegram.
I am not the she-bear taken as wife by a man.
I will not give birth to the bear boy hero
who'll save the tribe.
Take back your message
to the grandmothers who poke at the ashes
of my beginning-of-the-century thoughts.
Tell them to pack their travois of Arctic wind
and haul away the dull gray blades of these clouds.
Hurry on. Skip my generation of stars.
At the lip of spring
chapped by your kisses,
the numb thud of your heart stunning wisteria, tulips,
the bulging red buds of peonies,
time is short.
I fall daily in love with impossibilities—
the screech owl flying in front of the new moon,
the rufous hummingbird who puffs his throat
like a lung of electric carnelian
through the window,
the man shaped like a grizzly bear
but I know that
just as I feel my womb contract
troops are massing on the other side of the globe

for another war
too quick for even their long talons to stop.

From *Blood Flower*, first appeared in *Parnassus Review of Poetry*

THE HORSEMAN OF THE CRASS AND VULNERABLE WORD
    For Jim Harrison

The hemlock loses the tanager,
a bright blood streak
in a whirling gauze of snow.
Where do we go?
You told me the eye was lost,
old lens in a dish of milk
going to blue-veined cheese,
a lens that sneezed
when you laughed the mockingbird's laugh,
the horse's white laugh,
saying your brother accidentally
shot it out as you crawled
under barb wire, hunting.

I was young and fell in love
with your wounds, your tongue,
half-song, half-glands,
strong as the Calvinist hands
that whacked and fed your swampy youth.
I was young and drank vermouth
while you fell to your knees
in the Ford's back seat where you teased
until I laughed too much
when you begged please,
and your one-eyed touch
stared up at the night jar sky,
blinked at Orion, your
archer, saying good-bye.

I laughed but I feared your tongue,
your thighs. I was young.
I had heard.
Never love a poet at his word.

You were the man who could maim me
in those days when whiskey
clarified any dark thing.
Like Bobby and Annette we'd sing,
Baby, you're my beach blanket;
I'm your Mickey Mouse coquette.

You knew my crippled heart, my blind side
but I'd ride ride
ride on that edge where the heart's not given,
can't be taken
or lost to an archer or poet with one eye.
Oh, the heart has a spongy hide
believing in love's bromide.
Mine found its bed unmade, undone
when you left with your joking tongue.

But I tell you this now,
horseman of the crass and vulnerable word,
love is damp as a cloud-blown beach
and crawls in your bones
that never lose their ache.
When I dreamed your face—
so blindly polite, just the glimpse
of a lens of a face, just before
the horse, the dark and slippery horse I rode
so far out to sea
that the shore was a crumb the gulls couldn't eat—
I went numb in my sleep.
Even numbness passes.
I am half-blind in this half-blind night
but I've learned to ferment
wine from ash.

And you, it's always late—
you've broken your horse,
now lie under it.

From *Crazy Love* (2010 American Book Award), first appeared in *Another Chicago Magazine*

Nancy White

Nancy White's most recent poetry collection, *Detour*, was published by Tamarack Editions (March, 2010). Her first poetry collection, *Sun, Moon, Salt*, won the Washington Prize for Poetry in 1992.

White currently teaches English at Adirondack Community College, after previously teaching at St. Ann's School in Brooklyn and at Bennington College.

A graduate with an MFA from Sarah Lawrence College, White has been awarded fellowships at MacDowell and The Provincetown Arts Work Center. She serves as Associate Editor of *Sow's Ear Poetry Review* and also as Editor at Word Works in Washington, D.C.

© Nancy White

Derek Alger: Let me start by congratulating you on the recent publication of your poetry collection, Detour.

Nancy White: Well, it was a long wait! That book evolved over almost a decade, collecting more rejections than I can remember. My first book racked up a whopping 50-something before it won the Washington Prize, which got it into print, but I'd say *Detour* was at least double that. But I'm glad—looking back—that it took so long because I was forced to keep pressing the collection through the sieve of time and my own evolutions, and it really did improve every year it had to wait. It became more experimental, less narrative, and just plain more interesting. Or so I think…

DA: Did you really "write compellingly of love in all its true and skewered forms," as the blurb from Fred Marchant says?

NW: Skewered is a painful word isn't it? The poems are about divorce, in one sense, but also the collection is about the mid-life crisis everyone goes through in some form or another—we always find a way—and there's some painful skewering involved in those deconstructions and re-imaginings. One of the miracles of writing the poems, and of that phase of my life, really was that there was such genuine love that remained, and increased, after all the betrayal and cruelty and starting over. The human heart really is staggering in its goodness.

DA: Looks like you proved you can go home again.

NW: Metaphorically, and literally too! I wrote most of the book after leaving NYC to live near my large extended family upstate, in Cambridge, a small rural town where I run into people I went to high school with or who worked with my grandfather. To many NYC friends, it was shudderingly provincial, but for me it's an ideal place for writing, teaching, and community that reaches back not just years but many decades. I feel lucky to be reaping the benefits of continuity—living in my grandparents' old house, making parent complaints to the same school that irked me back in the day.

DA: Were your parents an influence on your desire to become a writer?

NW: Absolutely. My dad was in the Iowa MFA program, and there were always books around and people who loved them. My mom comes from a great storytelling tradition, plus she could get a cat talking, she's so good in conversation. We lived all over, and while that was traumatic in its way, it also loaded my mind with different places and people: Maine, Colorado, Vermont, Iowa, Wyoming, and we finally settled back in New York when I was a teenager.

DA: What about high school, did you start writing poetry early?

NW: I started out with melodramatic diary-keeping, then wrote bad stories with great seriousness of purpose, and in high school started writing poems. One great teacher is all it takes—and I was lucky to have one. Rumor had it she was an escaped nun, which I thought was gossip but later turned out to be true. She removed the pretense from the teacher-student relationship and cheerfully expected more than anyone ever had; the result was good writing from an astonishing number of students. She began my life-long love of metaphor.

But I got bored, as a lot of high school students do, so I graduated early, worked and traveled, writing most days, then went to Oberlin because it was the only place I hadn't visited, so it was the only place that hadn't made me nauseous.

DA: I hope Oberlin was a pleasant experience.

NW: The perfect blend of workaholic seriousness and freedom to explore. I loved it there. Though they really made you sweat to get into the writing classes—I had to wait two years. My advisor kept saying, "You're not ready to write. Go study history." The next semester, he'd say, "Go take science classes." Eventually he snuck me in the back door with the Translation Workshop, which I'm now convinced is the single most brilliant way to begin studying the construction of the poem and the mysteries of poetic voice. I did a shaggy variety of things at Oberlin, including getting up every day to fry eggs in the dining hall, starting a puppetry troupe, and working as an admissions intern.

DA: Your internship actually led to your first teaching job.

NW: I couldn't help but notice that all my favorite students came from the same school. They'd arrive for these interviews and the top of my head would fly off—so when the head of that school visited, I asked to be introduced to him, and he ended up saying I should come work for them. Serendipity?

DA: And it was another good experience?

NW: I think it formed me not only as a teacher but as a writer because the entire philosophy rubbed off on me. St. Ann's students typically studied the art of language more than anything else. Starting in 4th grade, students had two English courses, studio art taught by practicing artists, theater, plus science and history, and language and math taught by people passionate about the subject, with advanced degrees not in "education" but in the area they taught. By the end of high school, everyone had studied a modern and a classical language—sometimes

6 years of each. No grades were given, and you wouldn't believe how the students flourished. I taught creative writing there for a dozen years, inheriting students who had been reading and writing about and imitating the world's best writers ever since they could walk. Okay, I'm exaggerating…but only a little bit. The secret to their success was that the school knew, from top to bottom, that one of the teacher's most important jobs was knowing when to stay out of the way.

DA: You also earned an MFA from Sarah Lawrence.

NW: Yes, I sent myself to grad school because I thought I needed structure and deadlines, and after a review of the NYC programs, I picked Sarah Lawrence: great teachers, small classes, also the "don system," a one-on-one approach to complement the workshop. I have vivid memories of those hours, discussing a poem of mine that was failing, or that was half-hatched, and working it over with three different teachers in conference as well as in workshop. Plus that program demanded a long reading list and intensive study of our forebears every semester, so you came out with a balance of critical and creative skills. You can't earn a living as a poet in America now—or probably anytime soon—so it is a very pure education. You're not in it for the money but for its own sake.

DA: Eventually, it was time to move to upstate New York.

NW: I think I realized we had to go when my 9-month-old son crawled to the door and started banging on it with his fist. Since we'd been warned not to let him touch the ground in the park, or crawl on the restaurant floor, or touch the books at the library, we had to find a place that wasn't poisonous and where we all had more room to move. But also I could see the rest of my career stretching out ahead of me in a predictable manner, and I guess I prefer a little mystery, so I—I can't quite believe it now that I look back—turned away from Saint Ann's and after a couple of years at Bennington College moved into public higher education. A new set of frustrations, but a wonderful community of poets!

DA: *Tell us a bit about Women of Mass Dispersion.*

NW: Over the early years upstate, I kept meeting these very skilled women writers who were struggling to get published, who felt insecure or hampered when it came to getting their work into print. I was coming off a writing and publishing hiatus of my own, and I started tossing around the idea of meeting not so much as a writing group but as a publishing support group. We agreed to meet monthly to discuss writing projects, and to pool research and discuss strategy. One of the most important things we do is help each other meet our own personal deadlines and handle the many stings and arrows of rejection. Since we started, we've seen one member earn her MFA, several have received grants, numerous journal publications have resulted, several chapbooks and one book have come out, and with the mutual support, I think we've helped each other break some bad habits. And all this before Facebook!

DA: You're also involved with The Sow's Ear Poetry Review.

NW: Actually, I'm involved there because of a clerical error. I usually send out multiple submissions, and I accidentally sent poems to *Sow's Ear*, which was not accepting simultaneous submissions at that time, and another publication. The other publication accepted a poem, and then *Sow's Ear* wanted it too—and I didn't even have a record of sending it to them! I hadn't done it on purpose, apologized profusely, asked what I could do to make amends, suggesting I could help sort through any backlog if they had one. They auditioned me to read the slush pile, and I ended up as Associate Editor. Now, that includes writing  the book review column, which I love, love, love. It's an amazing way to keep up (or try to keep up) with new titles, meet new writers, and keep yourself thinking about the work that is coming out today.

DA: You're also Editor at Word Works.

NW: Yes. I won their Washington Prize years ago, and in 2008 I started working there, managing the prize process, moved on to editing and book production, then this January was elected president. My roles there are changing as fast as I can learn them—faster! Managing the prize process and then seeing the winner all the way through production is another way to see what's being written "out there," and then to get to know one excellent poet who has survived the grueling journey from slushpile to finalist to PRIZE. The president role really highlights the challenges that poetry is up against these days: so few readers, so little money, so little understanding of the mission of poetry—and yet so much potential, so many writers working to produce good books. It's both humbling and inspiring.

DA: Tell us about teaching at Adirondack Community College.

NW: I admire the mission of community college; it's vital to make quality education available to everyone, equally. We have a superb transfer program—really top-notch instruction—so that, yeah, you can use it as a trade school, but you can also use it to explore the power of the intellect, to explore creativity, to move beyond life-as-paycheck. A lot of our students are what we call "underprepared" for college, which is just the state of affairs in the U.S. right now, but I've seen amazing change in students in those two years. You can't help but feel you've struck a blow for civilization when a student enters as a future accountant, but ends up enrolled in a PhD program to study literature or psychology.

I do get to teach creative writing, but we all teach a mountain of college composition too. I love my department; they value the individual mind, the unique voice, not just the thesis statement and the ability to arrange yourself into paragraphs. This will sound inflated, but I really do think we restore our students' love of language, and their faith that it's a beautiful, powerful tool that belongs to each one of them inalienably.

DA: Whose poetry are you following these days?

NW: I like so many styles, kinds of voices. The irreverence and playfulness of someone like Daniel Nester, the rock-solid beauty of Deborah Digges, the always-forging-ahead Denise Duhamel, young poets like Judy Halebski …

In terms of "schools," I think "experimental" is the new cliché—every week I read another wandering volume by a writer whose publisher or blurber praises the work as "experimental." But the unintelligibility seems to me to be an enormous problem we need to address. Poetry already has a small enough audience these days!

I love the questing, austere bleakness of Julie Carr's *100 Notes on Violence*, which is one of the many so effusively dubbed experimental, but ... I think we need to be tougher about when it's important to share these experiments ("Look at me! Look at me!") and when it really is not. Maybe that's too esthetically pragmatic, my long-buried Puritanical roots showing, or something. But not everybody's uniquely textured inner playground is valuable as art.

A generation ago, the whining was about "too many confessional poets." And I know folks who are frustrated at the dominatrix presence of the lyric in recent years. Here's what one of last year's Washington Prize judges, Barbara Ungar, said when we were debating our final selection: "Which book would you return to in a time of need?" It became our definition of "important," and I think it transcends trends. I'll put it out there for comparison with other definitions of what makes poetry "good." Interestingly, while more of last year's finalists were lyric or narrative in nature (or some mixture therein), I'd say there is more experimental work in this year's finalist pile—using pretty much the same readers. Stay tuned for which book will be the 2010 volume.

Published in *Pif Magazine* August 6th, 2010

Poems by Nancy White

WOVEN AND SEWN

You are no virgin listen. You must stop here.
Sit on the curb and look like a bum.
Hold still until you feel it too.
There is a *no* rising in you like green sap like power.
Do not drill in your side. The world is not asking for this.
You are meant to stream upwards. No compromise only pause.
Sit in the dirt of the road until you see.
If it takes years it takes years.
This will cost less than the life you would drain from your side.
If you are hungry sleepless cold it is nothing to the other suffering.
There is no such *have* to that lie.
We once told it too. Don't be ashamed.
You are part of this fabric woven and sewn.
But not this what you contemplate willingly today.
You may hate us for these words. It passes.
Believe you are the one in danger. Sit down.

CORACLE

I was your coracle and you
slept, bobbing and sliding
on the sea. A few storms,
but we righted. You grew
to stretch from gunnel to gunnel,
then bow to stern. When we
tossed to shore and you rolled
onto the shingle rustling
and murmuring there, broken
teeth and the leathery hands
of centuries—history itself—
welcomed you. How light I was,

suddenly empty, all that
stretched space unneeded now
and the light blowing through
the skins of animals killed
to make me. Become drum. And
the smaller dints of stone lept up
on the wind to skip and flick,
rattle, stroke and sing
a while where you had been.
I became one of the lucky:
You carried me with you—easy,
maybe useful, on your shoulder.

THE OWL IN YOUR NAME

In the forest of ribs
no need to muster sky. She pulls the air behind her—
winging the breathable

world. Her job to stop
the small fast-beating ones, their twiggable limbs
and gray ribbons of fear. Their chittering
dissolves into stillness.

There's choice:
will you turn your name into the hole, all darkness
and no letters? Who would call for you
no longer if you did?

Answer it: what would yours
bring,
edible and open in her grip?

Bill Yarrow

Bill Yarrow is the author of *Blasphemer* (Lit Fest Press, 2015), *The Lice of Christ* (MadHat Press, 2014), *Incompetent Translations and Inept Haiku* (Červená Barva Press, 2013), and *Pointed Sentences* (BlazeVOX, 2012). His poems have appeared in *Poetry International, PANK, PIF Magazine, Del Sol Review, Contrary, DIAGRAM, Gargoyle, Uno Kudo, Confrontation*, and *RHINO*.
Yarrow is currently a Professor of English, serving as iCampus Faculty Coordinator from 2008-2014, at Joliet Junior College in Illinois, where he has taught since 1993, including courses in creative writing, Shakespeare, and film. He was a poetry editor at *THIS Literary Magazine* until it ceased publication in February 2013.

Derek Alger: Congratulations on the recent publication of your poetry collection, Pointed Sentences.

Bill Yarrow: Thanks, Derek. I'm very happy that Geoffrey Gatza and BlazeVOX published *Pointed Sentences* in January. It's a handsome volume and is a representative collection of 114 of my poems written mostly over the last three years—a prolific period in writing and publishing for me.

DA: The poet Tony Barnstone describes you as "the Sun Tzu of verbal warfare" and "the Machiavelli of mental strategy" in referring to Pointed Sentences.

BY: I appreciate Tony's comment and think it was very generous of him to say that. I think he's referring to the fact that my poems often pull the rug out from under the reader, move in unexpected directions, create a kind of reading and thinking whiplash. My poetic strategy seems to be that of the change-up, off-speed verbal pitches, an impetus to the unanticipated, continual (when I can manage it) surprise.

DA: You've published chapbook collections of poetry, but obviously with experience your poems are more accomplished now.

BY: There's no direct relationship between experience and accomplishment. It would be great if there were a constantly upward curve in terms of a writer's development, but it's not straightforward progress. Novice poets can write brilliant as well as jejune poems; experienced poets are quite capable of writing crap even at the height of their ability, even as they produce works of genius. Wordsworth is the perfect example of the inconsistent great poet. But if you mean that as experience fades and ripens, poets are better able to process experience and shape it into a successful story or poem, then I agree with you. And so did Wordsworth: "poetry is the spontaneous overflow of powerful feelings; it takes its origin from emotion recollected in tranquility." I completely agree with him. It takes me a long time—in some cases, decades—to process certain experiences. Tranquility can take a lifetime. With certain experiences, it may never come.

DA: As a kid, the word amusement had a different meaning for you than it had for many.

BY: Right! I grew up in an amusement arcade. My dad owned and ran a penny arcade on the boardwalk in Ocean City, Maryland, from 1947 to 1977. I spent every summer there, playing Skee-ball and pinball as a child, then working for my dad and running the business as I got older.

DA: You grew up in Philadelphia.

BY: Yes, we lived in the Philadelphia suburbs and my dad was home with us for most of the year. He went down to Ocean City in late May and my mom brought me and my three sisters down after school let out in June. We stayed down there for the summers and closed up in early September to return to Philadelphia for the start of public school.

DA: What were summers like at the amusement arcade?

BY: I met all kinds of colorful people and had a lot of singular experiences, but I look back on my summers mostly with horror. Ocean City is a wonderful place with a large, beautiful, white beach and much to offer. People who go there to vacation have a wonderful time. But when I was there, I didn't vacation; I worked—and not as a casual summer employee but as a permanent worker, the boss' son—and that made all the difference. Summers were traumatic for me. Working from 8:00 AM to midnight or 1:00 AM seven days a week all summer was grueling. Dealing with the arcade employees and with the customers (in this case, the entertainment-starved clientele that frequented a beach resort like Ocean City)  was a nightmare. At least it was for me. I was thankful when Ocean City ended—returning to high school and later college felt like an escape into paradise. I've just started in the last few years (that's over thirty years later!) to write about it. The handful of poems in *Pointed Sentences* that reference or directly confront Ocean City ("The Beaded Sheathe," "After the Shark," "Salt Thought," Great Moments in Blindness," Mussel Memory," "Ossian City," "George.") just begin to rattle the scab of the wound. I'm clearly not done with that subject in my poetry. In fact, I'm still processing a lot of those adolescent and post-adolescent experiences!

DA: I'm sure there are some good memories of Ocean City?

BY: MANY good memories. My best friend's father ran the frozen custard stand. We'd have free frozen custard at his dad's place and then go and play free pinball for hours and hours at my dad's. What could be better? Then we grew up. No one gets to stay in Eden forever.

DA: Fortunately, you were encouraged to read by your parents.

BY: Our house was *filled* with books. My dad was an amateur book collector, frequenting auction houses, buying up big lots of books of all kinds on all kinds of subjects. I read widely and ravenously. Maniacally! Since my dad was home during the school year, he and my mom often went to plays. Playbills everywhere!

DA: You were a natural for college.

BY: Environmentally favored and genetically predisposed. I was a good student. I went to Swarthmore College, where I took a lot of comparative literature classes, wrote poetry, won some prizes, got a degree in English literature.

DA: Being a poet was not as easy as you thought.

BY: No, but early encouragement goes a long way. It fuels me even today. There was a long stretch of years though when no one was interested in my poetry. I kept writing anyway.

DA: You ended up stepping out into the wider world.

BY: Along with everyone else.

DA: After college, you went to Israel soon after the Yom Kippur War and ended up as a volunteer on a kibbutz near the Lebanese border, and then traveled about Europe.

BY: So many people had similar if not identical experiences. I tried to write about this time in my life; I kept journals and filled notebooks, but I was unsuccessful. I didn't understand how to make use of my experience. I squandered a great opportunity. The first of many perhaps. Shakespeare has Richard II say, "I wasted time, and now doth time waste me." I came home with a lot of stories but ultimately empty handed and empty. I slumped back to Ocean City.

DA: One major opportunity wasn't squandered, you fell in love while corresponding with a woman you met on kibbutz.

BY: Yes, I did! And that was my salvation. But then love is everyone's salvation. Two writers fall in love through letters they write to each other. Imagine that! And then we got married a year and a half later over spring break in graduate school where she studied journalism and I got my MA in English literature, taking comprehensive exams in

Renaissance and 18th-century literature. Johnson and Boswell became late enthusiasms.

After graduation, we moved to New York, where I began teaching. And then we had two kids. And then we moved back to Chicago. And then I continued teaching. And then we had another kid. And then. And then. And here it is over thirty years later. And my kids are grown, and my wife and I just celebrated our thirty-sixth anniversary, and I am still teaching. Life. It's funny that way.

DA: How did you develop an interest in film?

BY: I was completely turned on by seeing films by Fritz Lang, Jean Renoir, Ernst Lubitsch, Jean-Luc Godard and others in T. Kaori Kitao's film study class at Swarthmore in 1972. Completely eye-opening and mind-blowing! I later took Alfred Appel's class in film noir at Northwestern. When I had the opportunity to teach film at Joliet Junior College, I grabbed it. I offer my film class each semester both in a face-to-face version and also online. I use a lot of public domain films (see The Internet Archive: www.archive.org). I'm a fanatic for film noir, silent films, and lesser known/obscure films (see my film blogs: http://byarrow.blogspot.com/ and http://billyarrow.blogspot.com/). Some of my favorites: *The Man Who Laughs* (Leni), *He Who Gets Slapped* (Sjostrom), *Cause for Alarm!* (Garnett), *The Man Who Cheated Himself* (Feist), *Woman on the Run* (Foster*)*, *Sudden Fear* (Miller), *The Blood of a Poet* (Cocteau), *Napoleon* (Gance), *La Chinoise* (Godard), *The Navigator* (Keaton), *Pickpocket* (Bresson), *The Red Shoes* (Powell), *Le Plaisir* (Ophuls), *Love Me Tonight* (Mamoulian), *Nazarin* (Bunuel), *Zoo in Budapest* (Lee). I like so many! Hard to pick.

DA: You also teach Shakespeare.

BY: And creative writing. And contemporary literature. And world literature. And composition. And developmental writing. I've taught (but which teacher hasn't?) many, many courses over the years.

DA: What relationship do you find between teaching and writing?

BY: Teaching allows you to understand the difference between the bad and the poor, between the poor and the good, between the good and the great. It educates your palate. It develops your taste. It forces you to cross borders. It requires you to think things through. It is simultaneously a telescope and a microscope. What I know about writing, I know from teaching. I don't believe in imitation but I do believe in models. I take ALL the great writing of the past as my model. I don't discriminate. I read everything and everyone. Writing is knowing. But I don't feel I really know anything until I've taught that thing. Teaching is humbling. It puts you face to face with greatness and dares you to back down. Writing is humbling too. It puts you face to face with what you know and dares you to walk away. I've tried not to walk away.

Published in *Pif Magazine* April 1st, 2012

Poems by Bill Yarrow

GEORGE

Skinny guy with glasses sent to Vietnam,
came back with an understanding of heroin,
an acquaintance with whorishness, a clarified
wife, and a helmet on his soul. His family alive
but indifferent, he makes his way back
to the ocean, back to the popcorn, back
to the pinball machines, wants to see
the boss who had treated him well. "Hey,
Bob! It's me, George!" Kindness is magnetic,
but the past is a loose adhesive and rarely
is employment a glue. "How nice to see
you, George!" He hangs around for about
an hour, then slinks back to the deserted
battlefield he has had tattooed on his future.

OSSIAN CITY

I can still hear
    the shriek
of the Laughing Lady,
    the crash
of a bucket of dimes,
    the waves
against the jetty at noon

I can still see the boardwalk
    empty with cyclists at 8 am,
at noon
    clogged with seagulls,
at midnight
    crowded with the ghosts
of sleeping old people

I can still hear
    the whir of rusted tackle
on the new marlin boat,
    the drip of cherry syrup
onto a cone of crushed ice,
    the scream of teens
dizzy for foam dice

I can still smell the greed
    of the hard sell,
fresh cigar ash in the sea,
    the mildewed freezer
in the dirty pool hall,
    the vinegar stink
of peanut-oil fries

I can still hear
    the sinister click
of Zippo lighters,

   the Chesterfield voices
of the Pokerino widows,
    the oily patter
of pock-faced shills

I can still taste the flounder chowder
    served by hairnet waitresses
to foul-mouthed barbers
    at City Lunch
while in the alley
    black men carted ice
on their backs with tongs

But most on sun-starved nights
I smell the foaming
    German shepherds
locked in cages
    under the pier
and the unworldly perfume
    of the pony-tailed girl
who played alone with darts

Derek Alger (18 Nov 1953–29 Oct 2014) was a graduate of the MFA fiction-writing program at Columbia University, a contributing editor for *Serving House Journal*, a non-fiction editor at *Ducts*, and a former editor-at-large at *Pif Magazine*, where more than 100 of his interviews with writers have been published over a period of 14 years. His fiction and essays appear in *Confrontation*, *Del Sol Review*, *Ducts.org*, *The Literary Review*, and *Writers Notes*, among others.

I

II

IN CHIESA PER 40 ANNI E NON CONOSCENDO *Dio*

Philip Guenaga

I contenuti di questa opera, inclusa, ma non limitata a, l'accuratezza degli eventi, delle persone e dei luoghi descritti; le opinioni espresse; il permesso di utilizzare materiali precedentemente pubblicati inclusi; e qualsiasi consiglio fornito o azione sostenuta sono di esclusiva responsabilità dell'autore, che assume tutta la responsabilità per l'opera suddetta e indennizza l'editore da qualsiasi pretesa derivante dalla pubblicazione dell'opera.

Tutti i diritti riservati.
Copyright © 2023 di Philip Guenaga

Nessuna parte di questo libro può essere riprodotta o trasmessa, scaricata, distribuita, sottoposta a reverse engineering o archiviata o introdotta in qualsiasi sistema di archiviazione e recupero delle informazioni, in qualsiasi forma o con qualsiasi mezzo, inclusa la fotocopiatura e la registrazione, sia essa elettronica o meccanica, ora nota o successivamente inventata, senza il permesso scritto dell'editore.

BRIMINGSTONE PRESS
WWW.BRIMINGSTONE.PRESS

ISBN: 978-1-953562-05-0

V

RICEVUTA

Ho conosciuto Philip Guenaga alcuni anni fa in una palestra che frequentavamo entrambi. Avevamo molto in comune quando parlavamo delle cose di Dio. Siamo diventati presto come fratello e sorella, anche se sai che non sono sempre d'accordo. Ma questa volta era diverso, le conversazioni erano stimolanti ed interessanti. Ognuno di noi condivideva la propria prospettiva su vari argomenti e a volte riprendevamo da dove avevamo lasciato il giorno prima. Mi è stato chiaro fin da quel momento quale passione Philip avesse per la Parola di Dio di cui discutevamo e abbiamo cominciato a canticchiare l'idea che lui scrivesse un libro. Ogni volta che ne parlavamo, mi faceva proprio tribolare. Mi ha dato diverse scuse su perché non potesse scrivere, su perché non fosse sicuro di dovrebbe farlo, e così via. Sono orgogliosa oggi di poter dire con entusiasmo che sono felice che abbia completato il libro che stai per leggere, e sono

emozionata che riceverai intuizioni che potresti non avere sperimentato prima.

Dott.ssa Precious Taylor

PREFAZIONE

Vorrei aggiungere una parola su questo libro e sull'autore. Conosco Philip Guenaga da 34 anni. Questo libro è innanzitutto un atto d'amore e in secondo luogo una vera comprensione della Parola di Dio. Philip ama il Signore al di là della comprensione umana. Questo libro è dedicato a coloro che cercano una relazione autentica con il Donatore della Vita, Gesù Cristo.

Da giovane, Philip ha avuto un'esperienza con Dio che lo ha sostenuto attraverso momenti difficili. Non ha mai dimenticato quell'esperienza, ovunque si trovasse. Quando Philip è arrivato a Rolla, nel Missouri, nel 1986 e ha frequentato la chiesa che pastoreggiavo, ho immediatamente visto la sua consacrazione. Per i successivi 2 anni e mezzo, è stato una grande benedizione per la nostra chiesa.

Credo di poter dire con fiducia che questo libro sarà una benedizione per te. Apri il tuo cuore mentre leggi questo libro e lascia che Dio ti parli.

Pastor Larry Thornhill

XI

TAVOLA DEI CONTENUTI

RICEVUTA VI

PREFAZIONE VIII

TAVOLA DEI CONTENUTI X

Introduzione XII

Il Vero Nome di Adamo ed Eva 4

La Vera Immagine di Dio 6

Incolpare la Donna 10

I Bambini nel Giardino dell'Eden 12

I Figli di Giobbe Non Furono Uccisi 18

Segni del Ritorno di Gesù Cristo 22

Il Piano di Salvezza...................................... 31

La Mia Testimonianza Personale................... 36

Ringraziamenti Personali 40

Bonus 41

IX

Introduzione

Permettimi di cominciare dicendo che c'è una enorme differenza tra conoscere Dio e conoscere di Dio. La maggior parte delle persone (soprattutto le persone religiose) conosce Dio solo superficialmente, ma pochi lo conoscono veramente.

Sono cresciuto con una madre molto religiosa. Nella Religione Cattolica mi hanno obbligato a fare la mia Prima Comunione e dopo di ciò mia madre ha avuto per la prima volta una Bibbia. Ha iniziato a leggerla e non era felice di ciò che leggeva perché non coincideva con ciò che le era stato insegnato. Da quel momento in poi, mia madre ci ha trascinato me e i miei fratelli attraverso varie religioni fino a quando non ha incontrato la dottrina Apostolica e

si è convertita a quella fede perché sentiva che fosse la dottrina più vicina alla Bibbia. Ovunque ci portasse, le storie della Bibbia non sono mai cambiate, è stato solo il "Piano di Salvezza" che cambiava da chiesa a chiesa o da religione a religione. Alcuni credevano che fosse necessario essere battezzati, mentre altri non erano d'accordo, alcuni non credevano che fosse necessario parlare in lingue, mentre altri dicevano che non si può essere salvati senza farlo.

Lo scopo principale di scrivere questo libro è provocarti nella speranza che tu legga la Bibbia da solo. Ti dimostrerò quanto poco conosci veramente Dio, indipendentemente dal tuo livello di istruzione riguardo alle Scritture.

IN CHIESA PER 40 ANNI E NON CONOSCENDO *Dio*

3

Il Vero Nome di Adamo ed Eva

Cominciamo con qualcosa di semplice, ogni religione a cui sono andato dice la stessa cosa: il NOME del primo uomo e della prima donna è Adamo ed Eva, se fai questa domanda nella tua chiesa nessuno sarà in disaccordo. C'è solo un problema, la Bibbia è in disaccordo. In Genesi 5:2 dice: "Li creò maschio e femmina e li benedisse, chiamandoli Adamo, il giorno in cui furono creati."

La Parola di Dio ci dice che li chiamò entrambi Adamo, Eva è il nome che l'uomo diede alla donna, non Dio, e l'uomo la chiamò inizialmente Donna prima di cambiarle il nome in Eva. Sì, so che la Bibbia fa riferimento in molte occasioni ad Adamo ed Eva, ma è qualcosa che l'uomo ha iniziato, non Dio. Ma nella perfetta Volontà di Dio sarebbero sempre stati Adamo. Se le cose sono cambiate, è

perché l'uomo ha apportato i cambiamenti, non Dio.

La Vera Immagine di Dio

Ciò porta a un'altra domanda: se Dio ha creato l'uomo (Adamo) a sua immagine, a chi si riferiva? All'uomo o alla donna? Entrambi furono chiamati Adamo e prima della caduta erano entrambi uguali agli occhi di Dio. Genesi 1:27 dice: "Dio creò l'uomo a sua immagine; a immagine di Dio lo creò; maschio e femmina li creò."

Non possiamo ignorare la fine di questo passo; entrambi furono creati a sua immagine, tuttavia Dio non ha un corpo, per così dire. Mi sono presentato davanti al Signore e così è andata la conversazione:

Io: Signore, chi è l'immagine? L'uomo e la donna sono immagini diverse.

Signore: Quali sono gli attributi di una donna?

Io: Per me, Signore, gli attributi di una donna sono amore, pazienza, longanimità, premura, per citarne alcuni.

Signore: E gli attributi di un uomo?

Io: Per me, Signore, gli attributi di un uomo sono legge, ordine, disciplina, correzione, per citarne alcuni.

Signore: Io sono tutto ciò, quindi solo nel matrimonio l'uomo diventa la mia immagine.

Ora, si può discutere che sto arrivando a una mia comprensione e che le Scritture non sono esattamente scritte in quel modo, ed è vero, ma puoi trovare passi delle Scritture per confutare ciò che ho appena scritto? O meglio, questa conversazione fa emergere altri passi delle Scritture?

Ad esempio, Genesi 2:24 dice: "Perciò l'uomo lascerà suo padre e sua madre e si unirà a sua moglie e diventeranno una sola carne."

Davvero credi che diventiamo una sola carne letteralmente? No, ma usando la comprensione di Dio, si riferisce alla sua immagine.

Un altro punto sull'immagine di Dio, potresti pensare che non abbia molta importanza, ma ti sbagli se lo pensi. L'immagine di Dio è una delle

forze più potenti qui sulla terra. Ricorda la storia in Matteo 8:28-34, parla di quei due posseduti da demoni che riconobbero in Gesù il Figlio di Dio, anche se Gesù non aveva ancora aperto la bocca, ed erano impauriti dal Signore. Per semplificarla, quante volte sei stato alla guida lungo la strada e hai visto una macchina della polizia o una pattuglia autostradale arrivare e hai frenato rapidamente anche se non stavi nemmeno velocizzando? È il rispetto per l'immagine e l'autorità che essa porta che ci fa reagire. Le coppie sposate dovrebbero capire che hanno anche quel tipo di rispetto e potere nel mondo spirituale e che i demoni dovrebbero temervi e rispettarvi quando vi vedono avvicinarsi. Matteo 18:19 dice: "Inoltre vi dico che, se due di voi concorderanno sulla terra per chiedere qualsiasi cosa, sarà fatta per loro dal Padre mio che è nei cieli." Questa è la ragione per cui Satana cerca sempre di distruggere i matrimoni, ha paura del potere che l'immagine ha. Se le coppie sposate (uomo e donna) si amassero davvero e fossero unite nell'accordo, Dio sarebbe vincolato alla sua Parola e i demoni tremerebbero.

Incolpare la Donna

In questo capitolo spiegherò come l'uomo abbia incolpato la donna per la caduta. Sin dai tempi più antichi, l'uomo ha sempre incolpato la donna per ciò che è accaduto nel Giardino dell'Eden. Sono qui per dirvi che non è mai stata colpa sua, è stata tutta colpa di Adamo. Esaminiamo attentamente Genesi 2:15-17, dove leggiamo che Dio aveva posto l'uomo nel giardino con l'istruzione di non mangiare dell'albero della conoscenza del bene e del male, e scopriremo anche che la donna non era ancora presente fino a Genesi 2:18-23. C'è qualcosa a cui dobbiamo prestare molta attenzione in Genesi 2:17: Dio non disse mai ad Adamo che non poteva toccare il frutto o l'albero, gli disse solo che non poteva mangiarne. Allora perché Eva dice al serpente in Genesi 3:3 che Dio aveva detto loro di non toccarlo? Dio non lo aveva detto ad Adamo e Eva non era presente durante quella conversazione, il che

significa che Adamo aveva trasmesso a Eva le informazioni su ciò che Dio aveva detto. Così, Adamo ha cambiato le parole di Dio aggiungendo che non potevano neanche toccarlo, mentendo sostanzialmente. È possibile che sia qui che Satana abbia trovato l'opportunità di attaccare la donna dato che le sono state fornite informazioni false? Dio diede istruzioni all'uomo, non alla donna, quindi quando la donna toccò il frutto, non accadde nulla e quando lo mangiò, non accadde nulla. Le istruzioni non erano per lei, ma solo per Adamo. Quindi, quando egli lo mangiò, i loro occhi furono aperti. L'ultima cosa che voglio fare è difendere il diavolo, ma ha davvero mentito quando disse a Eva che non sarebbero morti? Quando in realtà è stato Adamo a dire la bugia. Credo che se Adamo non avesse mangiato il frutto quando Eva lo fece, entrambi non sarebbero mai morti. Credo che Dio abbia punito Eva perché si è lasciata diventare uno strumento del diavolo nel convincere Adamo a mangiare il frutto.

Una nota veloce: il Signore disse ad Adamo che nel giorno in cui avrebbe mangiato il frutto sarebbe morto, molti faticano a capire questo poiché Adamo visse 930 anni. Vi spiegherò come Dio non ha mai torto: 2 Pietro 3:8 dice che un giorno presso il Signore è come mille anni e mille anni come un giorno. Quindi, Adamo non visse mai un intero giorno (mille anni), e morì lo stesso giorno.

I Bambini nel Giardino dell'Eden

Dato che siamo nel libro della Genesi, passiamo ora a qualcosa che tutte le chiese insegnano. Si suppone che Adamo ed Eva non abbiano avuto figli nel Giardino dell'Eden, esaminiamo da vicino ciò che le Scritture dicono.

Punto n. 1:

Genesi 1:28 E Dio li benedisse e Dio disse loro: Siate fecondi e moltiplicatevi, riempite la terra, soggiogatela e dominate sui pesci del mare, sugli uccelli del cielo e su ogni essere vivente che si muove sulla terra.

Devo credere che Adamo ed Eva sapevano come essere fecondi, altrimenti perché Dio darebbe loro un comandamento che non comprendevano? Non

sappiamo quanto tempo sono stati nel Giardino prima di essere cacciati, la Bibbia non lo dice.

Punto n. 2:

Genesi 3:16 Alla donna disse: Moltiplicherò i dolori delle tue gravidanze, partorirai con dolore; verso tuo marito sarà il tuo desiderio, ed egli ti dominerà.

Quando caddero, Dio punì Eva dicendole che i dolori del parto sarebbero aumentati notevolmente, doveva conoscere la differenza; se non avesse mai partorito prima, come avrebbe potuto sapere cosa aveva perso? Questo significa che aveva già partorito senza tanto dolore prima, quante volte non lo sappiamo, come ho detto, non sappiamo quanto tempo sono stati nel Giardino prima di essere cacciati. Inoltre, Dio l'aveva resa perfetta, quindi non avrebbe avuto problemi a rimanere incinta.

Punto n. 3:

Genesi 3:20 Adamo chiamò sua moglie Eva, perché essa è stata madre di tutti i viventi.

Adamo le cambiò il nome da "Donna" a "Eva" quando furono cacciati a causa di tutti i figli che aveva avuto, e l'unico modo per essere madre è partorire un figlio.

Punto n. 4:

Genesi 4:14 Ecco, tu mi cacci oggi da questo suolo e sarò nascosto dalla tua presenza; diventerò un errante e un vagabondo sulla terra, e chiunque mi troverà mi ucciderà.

Dopo che Caino uccise il fratello e Dio lo maledisse, Caino temeva che altri lo avrebbero ucciso. Chi lo avrebbe ucciso se fosse stato l'unico figlio sulla terra?

Punto n. 5:

Genesi 4:17 Caino conobbe sua moglie ed essa concepì e partorì Enoch; egli costruì una città e le diede il nome del figlio Enoch.

Caino aveva una moglie, da dove veniva? Possiamo davvero dire che Adamo ed Eva non hanno avuto figli nel Giardino dell'Eden, con tutte queste Scritture che dicono il contrario?

Punto n. 6:

Un ultimo punto, in Genesi 5:3 si dice che Adamo aveva 130 anni quando ebbe Set. Qualcuno mi spieghi perché ad Adamo ci sono voluti 130 anni per avere solo 3 figli. Sono nato nel 1960, i miei genitori sono stati sposati per circa 18 anni prima di divorziare e hanno avuto 8 figli. 130 anni e solo 3

14

figli, suvvia, qui c'è sicuramente qualcosa di sbagliato. E ricorda che Dio diede loro il comando di essere fecondi e moltiplicare la terra.

Spero che ora tu possa vedere perché sto cercando di spingere tutti a leggere la Bibbia da soli. Non puoi affidarti solo a chi si proclama qualche tipo di ministro quando essi stessi non studiano la Parola di Dio e passano solo studi che non hanno mai approfondito. E anche quando fai la ricerca, devi comunque rivolgerti all'Autore (Dio) per capire davvero appieno. È una buona cosa che Dio sia ancora qui e disponibile per chiedere aiuto.

Man mano che procederò, le cose diventeranno più sfidanti, ma farò del mio meglio con l'aiuto del Signore nostro Gesù Cristo per renderlo semplice da comprendere.

Ho già condiviso alcune delle mie comprensioni delle Scritture con studiosi della Bibbia e la loro risposta è che non importa se si crede che (Adamo ed Eva) abbiano avuto figli nel giardino o meno, non è così importante. Quanto è triste, quindi inventiamo storie mentre insegniamo la Parola di Dio al mondo, purché non influisca sul Piano di Salvezza, e ignoriamo le Scritture che dicono: Matteo 5:18 In verità io vi dico: finché non siano passati il cielo e la terra, non passerà neppure un iota o un trattino della Legge, senza che tutto sia compiuto. Tutto ciò che è scritto nella Bibbia è per

edificazione, il fatto che tu non abbia la comprensione completa non ti dà il diritto di svilirlo. Ora so da dove proviene Babbo Natale, dallo stesso posto da cui proviene l'Uovo di Pasqua. Dopotutto, quale danno c'è nel raccontare bugie in chiesa quando le storie sono carine e innocue? Inizi a capire perché nel mondo esistono così tante religioni?

Efesini 4:5 Un Signore, una fede, un battesimo, anche
Efesini 4:14 perché non siamo più bambini, sballottati e portati qua e là da ogni vento di dottrina, ingannati dagli uomini con l'astuzia, secondo un inganno diabolico.

I Figli di Giobbe Non Furono Uccisi

Questo prossimo punto probabilmente provocherà molta rabbia in molti ministri poiché rifiuteranno di credere di aver insegnato e predicato questa storia in modo errato. La storia di Giobbe, tutti credono che Dio abbia permesso a Satana di uccidere i figli di Giobbe, ma la verità è che i figli di Giobbe non sono mai stati uccisi. Dovrò condurti nella scrittura originale ebraica per capire. Non so perché il traduttore abbia fatto così, ma qui è iniziato il problema. Quando leggiamo la storia di Giobbe e iniziamo a leggere come ha iniziato a perdere le sue ricchezze, dobbiamo prestare molta attenzione alla parola "servo".

Questi sono i due tipi di parole ebraiche e le relative definizioni della parola "servo":

(1) eh'-bed, servo: - X schiavitù, schiavo, (uomo-) servo.

(2) nah'-ar, dall'età dell'infanzia all'adolescenza; per implicazione un servo; anche (per interscambio di sesso) una ragazza (di età simile): - bambino, ragazzo, fanciulla [dalla nota], giovane (uomo) servo.

Giobbe 1:8 E l'Eterno disse a Satana: «Hai notato il mio servo Giobbe? Non c'è nessuno come lui sulla terra: uomo integro e retto, che teme Dio e si allontana dal male».

Giobbe 1:15 I Sabei si sono gettati su di loro, li hanno rapiti e hanno ucciso a colpi di spada i servitori (nah'-ar); solo io sono scampato per dirtelo.

Giobbe 1:16 Mentre costui stava ancora parlando, un altro arrivò e disse: «Dal cielo è caduto il fuoco di Dio, ha divorato le pecore e i servi (nah'-ar) e li ha consumati; solo io sono scampato per dirtelo».

Giobbe 1:17 Mentre costui stava ancora parlando, un altro arrivò e disse: «I Caldei, divisi in tre schiere, si sono gettati sui cammelli e li hanno portati via, e hanno ucciso a colpi di spada i servitori (nah'-ar); solo io sono scampato per dirtelo».

Giobbe 1:18 Mentre costui stava ancora parlando, un altro arrivò e disse: «I tuoi figli e le tue figlie stavano mangiando e bevendo vino nella casa del loro fratello maggiore;

Giobbe 1:19 ed ecco, un gran vento è venuto dal deserto, ha colpito le quattro angoli della casa, ed essa è crollata sui giovani (nah'-ar), che sono morti; solo io sono scampato per dirtelo.

In Giobbe 1:8 la parola "servo" si riferisce a "eh'-bed", che è un uomo schiavo. Ma quando entriamo nella storia in cui i servitori si avvicinano a Giobbe e gli riferiscono gli incidenti, Giobbe 1:15-19, ogni volta che vedi la parola "servitore", è la traduzione di "nah'-ar" che si riferisce a un bambino, non a un uomo schiavo. E qui è dove il traduttore commette un errore molto grave. In Giobbe 1:19 dove è scritto "ed è caduta sui giovani" o in ebraico "nah'-ar", perché il traduttore ha scelto di usare una traduzione diversa dopo aver iniziato con "servitore" (nah'-ar)? Perché non "bambino", "ragazzo", "bambino", "fanciulla"? Sono tutte traduzioni corrette, ma poiché ha usato una parola diversa, fa pensare a tutti che si stia riferendo a qualcosa di diverso quando non è così. Se il traduttore avesse iniziato con "giovani" e avesse concluso con "giovani", nessuno avrebbe pensato che si riferisse ai figli di Giobbe. Ma poiché ha iniziato con "servitori", avrebbe dovuto finire con

"servitori" e non concludere usando la parola "giovani".

Senza considerare che i figli di Giobbe erano tutti adulti, la Bibbia dice che stavano tutti bevendo vino, i bambini non bevono vino, e tutti i servi di Giobbe erano dall'età dell'infanzia all'adolescenza. Un altro punto è che se i figli di Giobbe fossero stati uccisi, perché sua moglie sarebbe stata d'accordo? Non sembrava importarle finché Satana non toccò il corpo di Giobbe, allora lei perse la calma e disse a Giobbe di maledire Dio e morire. Suppongo che si preoccupasse di più del corpo di Giobbe che dei suoi stessi figli.

Segni del Ritorno di Gesù Cristo

Il prossimo argomento che cercherò di affrontare sarà il più impegnativo. Richiederà molte Scritture, il che è positivo perché lo renderà ancora più solido e confermato. Tratterà della venuta del nostro Signore Gesù Cristo, tuttavia, desidero informarvi che alcuni già credono come faccio io, mentre altri sono completamente contrari. La maggior parte delle persone crede che i Sigilli scritti nel libro dell'Apocalisse non siano ancora aperti e che non si apriranno fino dopo il rapimento della Chiesa. Dimostrerò che al momento attuale sono stati aperti cinque sigilli. Dovremo andare al libro di Matteo 24:3-35 o Marco 13:3-37, scegliete voi, preferisco Matteo. Allo stesso tempo, dovete aprire la vostra Bibbia ai capitoli 6 e 7 dell'Apocalisse, è meglio se avete a disposizione due Bibbie poiché sarà più

facile saltare da Matteo (o Marco) all'Apocalisse per fare i confronti che indicherò.

Il primo punto che dobbiamo riconoscere è che in Matteo 23:3 gli apostoli volevano sapere i segni della sua venuta e quando sarebbe avvenuta la fine del mondo. Lo chiedono a Gesù e il Signore comincia a parlare loro dei segni da cercare. Da questo momento in poi, dobbiamo accettare che tutto ciò che Gesù dice è in riferimento ai segni del suo ritorno e alla fine del mondo. Matteo 24:4 E Gesù rispose e disse loro: "Fate attenzione che nessuno vi inganni.

Matteo 24:5 Perché molti verranno nel mio nome, dicendo: "Io sono il Cristo"; e inganneranno molti. Ora passiamo a Apocalisse 6:2 E vidi, ed ecco un cavallo bianco; e colui che sedeva sopra di esso aveva un arco, e una corona gli fu data; ed egli uscì per vincere e per vincere. Per coloro che non ne sono a conoscenza, il nostro Signore sta tornando su un cavallo bianco e con molte corone (Apocalisse 19:11 – 16). Quindi, come potete vedere, l'individuo descritto nel primo sigillo dà l'impressione di essere una specie di Cristo. E il primo peccato commesso fu quando Satana prese la Parola di Dio e la distorta per ingannare Eva nel Giardino, e Satana ha continuato a farlo da allora. Ha persino cercato di ingannare Gesù nel deserto cercando di distorcere le Scritture per far sì che Gesù trasformasse le pietre in pane. Questo è il primo segno, Satana esce per conquistare e

conquistare. Un altro punto veloce è che 1 Pietro 5:8 dice che Satana è come un leone ruggente, ma in Apocalisse 5:5 dice che Gesù è il leone. Satana cerca sempre di imitare Gesù. Questa è la ragione per cui ci sono così tante religioni, la principale arma di Satana è la religione per ingannare le persone a credere di essere salvate.

Ora, alcuni studiosi potrebbero sfidare la mia interpretazione di questo primo sigillo e va bene, perché il punto che sto cercando di dimostrare è che i primi cinque sigilli sono aperti indipendentemente dal loro significato. Sono sicuro di avere ragione, però.

Non proverò a dare un'interpretazione esatta per ciascun sigillo, ma farò notare che ogni volta che un sigillo si apre, noterete che stiamo già vivendo ciò che è scritto nei primi cinque sigilli.

Il secondo sigillo (2° segno) si apre in Apocalisse 6:3 E quando egli ebbe aperto il secondo sigillo, udii il secondo animale dire: "Vieni e vedi".

Apocalisse 6:4 E uscì un altro cavallo, rosso; e fu dato a colui che sedeva sopra di esso di togliere la pace dalla terra, e che dovessero uccidersi a vicenda; e gli fu data una grande spada. Possiamo paragonare questo a ciò che il Signore disse ai suoi discepoli in Matteo 24:6 E udrete di guerre e di voci di guerre; guardate di non spaventarvi; perché queste cose devono accadere, ma la fine non è ancora.

Passiamo ora al terzo sigillo (3° segno), Apocalisse 6:5 E quando egli ebbe aperto il terzo sigillo, udii il terzo animale dire: "Vieni e vedi". Ed ecco, un cavallo nero; e colui che sedeva sopra di esso aveva una bilancia in mano.

Apocalisse 6:6 E udii una voce in mezzo agli esseri viventi dire: "Un chilo di grano per un denaro e tre chili d'orzo per un denaro; ma non danneggiare l'olio e il vino". Questo sigillo parla di carestie e in Matteo 24:7 il Signore parla anche di carestie come segno.

Passiamo ora al quarto sigillo (4° segno), Apocalisse 6:7 E quando egli ebbe aperto il quarto sigillo, udii la voce del quarto animale dire: "Vieni e vedi".

Apocalisse 6:8 E vidi, ed ecco un cavallo pallido; e colui che sedeva sopra di esso si chiamava Morte, e l'inferno lo seguiva. E fu dato loro potere sulla quarta parte della terra, per uccidere con la spada, con la fame, con la morte, e con le bestie della terra. Questo sigillo sembra molto simile a ciò che il Signore dice ai discepoli in Matteo 24:7.

Passiamo ora al quinto sigillo (5° segno), Apocalisse 6:9 E quando egli ebbe aperto il quinto sigillo, vidi sotto l'altare le anime di coloro che erano stati uccisi per la Parola di Dio e per la testimonianza che avevano.

Apocalisse 6:10 E gridavano a gran voce, dicendo: "Fino a quando, Signore santo e verace, non giudichi e vendichi il nostro sangue su quelli che abitano sulla terra?

Apocalisse 6:11 E furono date loro delle vesti bianche, e fu detto loro di riposare ancora un poco, finché fossero compiuti anche i loro compagni di servizio e i loro fratelli, che dovevano essere uccisi come erano stati loro. Fate attenzione a ciò che il Signore dice ai suoi discepoli dopo, Matteo 24:9 Allora vi consegnaranno per essere afflitti e vi uccideranno; e sarete odiati da tutte le nazioni a causa del mio nome. Qualcuno può davvero negare che questi sigilli siano ancora chiusi? Siamo testimoni di queste attività che accadono ancora oggi. La storia della Bibbia mostra che tutti questi segni sono avvenuti in sequenza corretta. Il prossimo sigillo (6°) è ancora chiuso ed è uno studio completamente diverso. Molti saranno in disaccordo con me, se non lo sono già, ma ancora una volta farò del mio meglio per non offendere il mio Signore Gesù Cristo.

È nel sesto sigillo che iniziano a verificarsi cose terribili che non abbiamo ancora visto.

Apocalisse 6:12 E io vidi, quando egli ebbe aperto il sesto sigillo, ed ecco, ci fu un grande terremoto; e il sole divenne nero come sacco di capelli, e la luna divenne come sangue;

Apocalisse 6:13 E le stelle del cielo caddero sulla terra, come un fico getta i suoi fichi prematuri quando è scosso da un vento potente.

Apocalisse 6:14 E il cielo si ritrasse come un rotolo quando viene arrotolato; e ogni montagna e isola fu rimossa dal suo posto.

Apocalisse 6:15 E i re della terra, i grandi uomini, i ricchi, i capitani e i potenti, e ogni servo e ogni libero, si nascosero nelle caverne e nelle rocce delle montagne;

Apocalisse 6:16 E dicevano ai monti e alle rocce: "Cadete su di noi, e nascondeteci dal volto di colui che siede sul trono e dalla collera dell'Agnello;

Apocalisse 6:17 Perché il grande giorno della sua ira è venuto; e chi sarà in grado di resistere?"

Ora saltiamo a Matteo e leggiamo ciò che Gesù dice ai suoi discepoli

Matteo 24:21 Poiché in quei giorni ci sarà una grande tribolazione, quale non vi è stata dal principio del mondo fino a ora, né mai vi sarà.

Matteo 24:22 E se quei giorni non fossero abbreviati, nessuna carne sarebbe salvata; ma a causa degli eletti quei giorni saranno abbreviati.

Matteo 24:23 Allora, se qualcuno vi dirà: "Ecco, qui è il Cristo", o "Là", non lo crediate.

Matteo 24:24 Perché sorgeranno falsi Cristi e falsi profeti, e faranno grandi segni e prodigi, tanto da ingannare, se possibile, anche gli eletti.

Matteo 24:25 Ecco, vielo ho predetto.

Matteo 24:26 Perciò, se vi diranno: "Ecco, egli è nel deserto", non uscite; o "Ecco, egli è nelle stanze segrete", non lo crediate.

Matteo 24:27 Poiché come il lampo esce dall'est e risplende fino all'ovest, così sarà anche la venuta del Figlio dell'uomo.

Matteo 24:28 Poiché dovunque sarà il cadavere, ivi si raduneranno gli avvoltoi.

Matteo 24:29 Ma subito dopo la tribolazione di quei giorni, il sole sarà oscurato, e la luna non darà la sua luce, e le stelle cadranno dal cielo, e le potenze dei cieli saranno scosse;

Matteo 24:30 E allora apparirà il segno del Figlio dell'uomo nei cieli; e allora tutte le tribù della terra faranno lamento, e vedranno il Figlio dell'uomo venire sulle nubi del cielo con potenza e grande gloria.

Matteo 24:31 Ed egli manderà i suoi angeli con gran suono di tromba, e raduneranno i suoi eletti dai quattro venti, da un'estremità del cielo all'altra.

Spero davvero che ora possiate vedere che Gesù sta condividendo con i suoi discepoli ciò che è scritto nei primi sei sigilli. Molti predicatori insegnano che la Chiesa non attraverserà una tribolazione, ma ovviamente si sbagliano. Gesù non appare fino dopo la grande tribolazione. Come potete leggere in Matteo 24:29, coincide con Apocalisse 6:12 e 13, ed è in Matteo 24:31 quando Gesù finalmente raduna la sua Chiesa. Nel libro dell'Apocalisse, ciò avviene solo nel capitolo 7:9. Per coloro che non accettano che questa sia la Chiesa, devono professare che ci saranno due rapimenti, non uno solo, perché la Chiesa è l'unica che ha lavato le sue vesti nel sangue dell'Agnello. Lo si trova in Apocalisse 7:14 e dice anche che questi sono quelli che sono usciti dalla Grande Tribolazione.

Fidatevi di me, quando sentite i predicatori predicare che viviamo negli ultimi giorni, sono perfettamente in linea. Non abbiamo idea di quando si aprirà il sesto sigillo. Potremmo non conoscere il giorno o l'ora della sua venuta, ma lo sapremo quando si presenterà il sole nero, la luna rossa e le stelle cadranno dal cielo. Gioele 2:31 "Il sole si muterà in tenebre e la luna in sangue, prima che venga il giorno grande e terribile del Signore".

E Atti 2:20 "Il sole si muterà in tenebre e la luna in sangue, prima che venga il giorno grande e notabile del Signore". Sarà l'ultima volta che ci inginocchieremo e chiederemo perdono a Dio e lui ci perdonerà affinché siamo senza macchia o ruga proprio prima che siamo rapiti. Si adempirà la Scrittura di Efesini 5:27 affinché egli stesso possa presentare a se stesso una Chiesa gloriosa, non avendo macchia, ruga o alcuna cosa simile; ma affinché sia santa e senza difetto. Tuttavia, ciò si applicherà solo a coloro i cui nomi sono scritti nel Libro della Vita.

Luca 10:20 Tuttavia, non rallegratevi perché gli spiriti vi sono soggetti, ma rallegratevi piuttosto perché i vostri nomi sono scritti nei cieli.

Apocalisse 20:15 E chiunque non fu trovato scritto nel libro della vita fu gettato nel lago di fuoco.

Il Piano di Salvezza

C'è solo un modo in cui si può avere il proprio nome scritto nel libro della vita.

Giovanni 3:1 C'era un uomo dei farisei di nome Nicodemo, un principe dei Giudei.

Giovanni 3:2 Egli venne da Gesù di notte e gli disse: «Rabbì, sappiamo che tu sei un maestro venuto da Dio; infatti nessuno può fare questi segni che tu fai se Dio non è con lui».

Giovanni 3:3 Gesù rispose e gli disse: «In verità, in verità ti dico: se uno non è nato di nuovo, non può vedere il regno di Dio».

Giovanni 3:4 Nicodemo gli disse: «Come può un uomo nascere quand'è vecchio? Può forse entrare

una seconda volta nel grembo di sua madre e nascere?».

Giovanni 3:5 Gesù rispose: «In verità, in verità ti dico: se uno non è nato d'acqua e di Spirito, non può entrare nel regno di Dio.

Giovanni 3:6 Quel che è nato dalla carne è carne, e quel che è nato dallo Spirito è spirito.

Giovanni 3:7 Non meravigliarti se ti ho detto: dovete nascere di nuovo.

Giovanni 3:8 Il vento soffia dove vuole e ne odi il suono, ma non sai da dove viene né dove va. Così è di chiunque è nato dallo Spirito».

Gesù rende molto chiaro che c'è solo un modo per entrare nel regno di Dio, non diversi. Vuoi trasferirti da lui quando muori? Allora devi nascere di nuovo, d'acqua e di Spirito. Il Signore Gesù Cristo disse ai suoi discepoli di andare e insegnare a tutte le nazioni, battezzandoli nel nome del Padre, del Figlio e dello Spirito Santo (Matteo 28:19). Ora, per coloro che praticano il battesimo per immersione completa nell'acqua, state iniziando bene, ma state solo diventando bagnati se prima non vi siete pentiti dei vostri peccati. Inoltre, il ministro che ti sta battendo deve invocare il nome di Gesù Cristo. Sì, Gesù Cristo, e non Padre, Figlio e Spirito Santo, perché questi sono titoli, non un nome. Leggi

attentamente la Scrittura e noterai che Gesù dice di battezzare nel nome, non nei nomi, il nome del Padre è Gesù (Giovanni 5:43 Sono venuto nel nome di mio Padre, e voi non mi avete accolto; se un altro viene nel proprio nome, voi lo accoglierete), il nome del Figlio è Gesù, e il nome dello Spirito Santo è Gesù (Giovanni 14:26 Ma il Consolatore, lo Spirito Santo, che il Padre manderà nel mio nome, quello vi insegnerà ogni cosa e vi ricorderà tutto ciò che vi ho detto). Perché quando preghiamo, preghiamo sempre nel nome di Gesù, ma quando si tratta del battesimo, molti dicono Padre, Figlio, Spirito Santo? Non c'è altro nome per cui dobbiamo essere salvati.

Atti 4:12 E in nessun altro c'è salvezza, perché non c'è altro nome sotto il cielo dato agli uomini, mediante il quale possiamo essere salvati.

La sposa assume sempre il nome dello sposo. Padre, Figlio e Spirito Santo non sono nomi. E se non lo hai notato nel libro degli Atti, tutti gli apostoli battezzarono nel nome del Signore nostro Gesù Cristo.

Passiamo ora a essere nati di nuovo nello Spirito. Molti non comprendono la Scrittura di Giovanni 3:8. Gesù sta spiegando come il vento soffia e lo sentiamo, e alla fine dice "così è chiunque è nato dello Spirito". Non so tu, ma io posso anche stare all'interno di un edificio, guardare fuori e vedere se

il vento soffia guardando gli alberi e i cespugli, e posso anche uscire fuori e sentire il vento soffiare. Gesù non sta parlando di vedere o sentire il vento soffiare. Sta parlando di sentire il vento soffiare, c'è un suono, che coincide con il giorno di Pentecoste, quando tutti parlavano in lingue quando lo Spirito Santo scese su di loro. Atti 2:2 E improvvisamente venne dal cielo un suono come di vento impetuoso... Quindi, se dici di avere ricevuto lo Spirito Santo, deve essere attraverso l'evidenza del parlare in altre lingue, perché deve essere udito (un suono), non sentito o visto. Ancora una volta Gesù disse: "così è chiunque è nato dello Spirito", non alcuni, non solo questa generazione, o solo gli apostoli o i discepoli... OGNIUNO.

Qualcuno potrebbe dire, come si fa a ricevere lo Spirito Santo, piuttosto semplice in realtà. È un dono da Dio, nessun lavoro richiesto, nessun digiuno o riti speciali, solo credere. Se già credi in Dio senza averlo mai visto, allora hai già molta fede per ricevere lo Spirito Santo. Parla in lingue come ti guida il Signore, mentre parli in lingue e credi che sia lo Spirito Santo, allora è lo Spirito Santo, se credi che stai fingendo, allora stai fingendo, è totalmente basato sulla tua fede e su nessun altro. Nessuno dovrebbe poterti convincere che Dio non esiste, e nessuno dovrebbe poterti convincere che non hai lo Spirito Santo se hai parlato in lingue. Molti ti chiederanno se hai sentito qualcosa, ma i sentimenti non c'entrano nulla. Mi alzo al mattino

ogni giorno e raramente sento la presenza del Signore, vuol dire che non esiste? Questo è cruciale nella tua camminata con Dio, l'unico modo per sopravvivere è imparare a camminare per fede, altrimenti il nemico ti distruggerà. Questa è una delle, se non la principale ragione per cui andiamo in chiesa. Per rafforzare la nostra fede, non hai bisogno di andare in chiesa per sentirti dire di non mentire, imbrogliare, rubare, ecc. Questo dovresti già saperlo.

Per favore, sappi che non sto promuovendo alcuna religione, se sei felice dove sei, allora rimani lì. Sto solo cercando di assicurarmi che tu capisca come far scrivere il tuo nome nel libro della Vita. Se il tuo Padre Celeste non è contento di dove ti trovi, quella è una questione tra te e Lui, sono solo un servo che cerca di amare tutti indipendentemente da dove adorino.

La Mia Testimonianza Personale

Sto per condividere un po' di più della mia testimonianza, poiché ho già condiviso all'inizio come sono cresciuto con una madre molto religiosa. C'era un'atmosfera infernale in casa, l'amore non esisteva nella mia famiglia. Ho un fratello maggiore e cinque sorelle, e ci odiavamo tutti reciprocamente. Gli abusi che ho subito da bambino mi avrebbero fatto desiderare di essere stato abortito. Quando il Signore finalmente ha fatto il suo impatto su di me all'età di 17 anni e ho fatto penitenza e ho voluto essere battezzato, l'ho detto a mia madre e lei mi ha detto che ero un idiota e che non sapevo cosa stessi facendo. Inutile dire che non è venuta al mio battesimo, anche se è stata lei a portarmi in chiesa all'inizio. Non farmi parlare di mio padre, era solo un donatore di sperma. Ci avrebbe picchiato ogni volta che ne aveva

l'opportunità, che lo meritassimo o no, e Dio ci aiutasse se un vicino venisse a lamentarsi di noi, perché ci avrebbe picchiato fino a farci sanguinare di fronte al vicino. Non avevo autostima, la mia media scolastica da senior al liceo era di 1,67. Non so nemmeno come sia riuscito a diplomarmi. Non ho mai saputo cos'era l'amore fino a quando ho dato la mia vita a Dio, anche ora ho ancora problemi a causa di ciò, eppure il mio amorevole Dio mi ha benedetto con la moglie migliore e più bella del mondo. Mi sono sposato all'età di 31 anni, un'attesa che ne è valsa la pena. Ho servito 10 anni nell'esercito. Per favore, non sentirti dispiaciuto per me, ci sono molti bambini che hanno avuto situazioni peggiori della mia, sono solo grato che il Signore non si sia stancato di bussare alla mia porta finché non ho risposto. Il Signore mi ha usato per pregare per i malati e mi ha persino fatto pregare per un uomo morto che è tornato in vita. Ho avuto esperienze fuori dal corpo, sogni, visioni... ecc. Conosco il mio Dio, sono persino arrivato a un punto quando ero giovane nella fede e volevo mettere fine alla mia vita perché sentivo di non avere un amico, e Dio è apparso e mi ha detto che sarebbe stato il mio amico, la mia vita non è mai stata la stessa da allora.

Non so cos'altro posso scrivere per spingere tutti a leggere di più la Bibbia, so che non è facile da capire, ma più la leggerai, più inizierai a capire Dio. Ci sono state volte in cui ho letto la Bibbia e ho

trovato difficile credere che Dio avrebbe fatto certe cose, e più la studio, più comprensione ho ottenuto. A volte ci vogliono anni per ottenere una rivelazione, e sì, la rivelazione viene solo da Dio se gli aggrada rivelartela. Ad esempio, in Luca 7:19-22, ho trovato difficile credere la risposta che Gesù ha dato ai discepoli da dare al suo cugino Giovanni, che era rinchiuso in prigione, riguardo ai miracoli che aveva compiuto, riguardo ai ciechi che potevano vedere, ai claudi che camminavano e ai lebbrosi che venivano purificati, e ai morti che venivano risuscitati. E allora? Anche Satana ha il potere di guarire (Apocalisse 13:3 E uno dei suoi capi sembrava colpito a morte, ma la ferita mortale gli fu rimarginata. E tutto il mondo andava dietro alla bestia con meraviglia.). Ho lottato con questo per anni finché il Signore non ha aperto i miei occhi: Gesù non si riferiva ad esso come un aspetto fisico, ma lo ha riferito da una prospettiva spirituale. È venuto a salvare ciò che era perduto (Matteo 18:11), il suo popolo aveva occhi ma non poteva vedere e perché non potevano vedere, non potevano camminare, i lebbrosi purificati si riferiscono ai loro peccati perdonati e i morti spiritualmente risuscitavano, e questo è qualcosa che Satana non può fare. Questo va direttamente alle Scritture Isaia 55:8 Poiché i miei pensieri non sono i vostri pensieri, né le vostre vie sono le mie vie, dice il Signore. Isaia 55:9 Come i cieli sono più alti della terra, così le mie vie sono più alte delle vostre vie e i miei pensieri delle vostre pensieri.

L'unico modo in cui capiremo alcune delle cose scritte nella Bibbia è se piace a Dio darci la sua comprensione. Va bene se non capisci le Scritture, dovresti almeno parlare con Lui per chiedere aiuto. È più che disposto a condividere, ciò che rende difficile capire è quando gli uomini ti riempiono della loro comprensione, ognuno ha un'opinione, da qui le numerose religioni. Stabilisci una vita di preghiera, chiunque non sappia leggere può comunque conoscerlo, parla con lui, è così che ho scoperto tutto ciò che ho scritto in questo libro, parlando con Lui e chiedendogli.

Ringraziamenti Personali

Voglio esprimere un ringraziamento speciale al mio Pastore Larry Thornhill, che mi ha guidato quando ero di stanza a Ft. Leonard Wood, in Missouri. È lui che mi ha incoraggiato a scrivere. Voglio anche ringraziare la mia amica speciale Dott.ssa Precious Taylor, che mi ha spinto a scrivere ed è andata oltre per editare il mio libro. E naturalmente, la mia adorabile moglie Reyna Guenaga, che ha realizzato tutte le illustrazioni.

Grazie a tutti voi e vi amo tutti,

Il vostro umile servo,

Philip Guenaga

Bonus

Ciò che sto per condividere con voi riguarda la mia personale teoria sui dinosauri. So che molte persone si chiedono dove si inseriscano nella creazione e nell'esistenza dell'uomo. Non possiamo negare che essi non esistano perché i musei sono pieni di prove, eppure gli scienziati sostengono che abbiano milioni di anni e secondo la Bibbia, l'uomo esiste solo da 6.000 a 7.000 anni. Lasciate che vi spieghi utilizzando le Scritture.

Genesi 1:1 Nel principio Dio creò i cieli e la terra.

Genesi 1:2 La terra era informe e deserta, e le tenebre erano sulla faccia dell'abisso, e lo Spirito di Dio aleggiava sulla faccia delle acque.

Come potete vedere, nella Genesi 1:1 si parla di una creazione, ma nel secondo verso non c'è nulla. Se vi dico che ho costruito una casa e vi mostro un terreno vuoto, mi chiederete dov'è la casa. Stessa cosa qui, dov'è la creazione? Credo che qualcosa sia successo tra i versetti 1 e 2. Notate anche che la terra era in presenza di Dio fin dall'inizio, non è stato fino al secondo giorno della creazione che Dio ha allontanato la terra dalla sua presenza creando un firmamento tra sé stesso e la terra, vedere Gen. 1:6-8.

Se andiamo a Ezechiele 28:11-19 leggeremo di un cherubino unto che è stato cacciato, altrimenti noto come Satana. Afferma che questo cherubino prima di essere cacciato camminava nell'Eden (Eze. 28:13). Come è possibile? Sappiamo che lui era lì dopo la caduta come serpente, ma è scritto che lui era lì prima della caduta. Ci sono stati due Giardini dell'Eden? Non credo!

Credo che la prima creazione che Dio ha creato in Gen. 1:1 appartenesse a Lucifero (Lucifero disse che avrebbe innalzato il suo trono sopra le stelle di Dio Isa. 14:13), un trono rappresenta un regno, ed è qui che Dio ha creato la prima creazione per questo cherubino speciale (Lucifero) insieme ai dinosauri, proprio come Dio ha creato tutti gli animali che esistono oggi per Adamo. Ma quando fu trovata iniquità in lui, il Signore lo allontanò dal cielo e lo cacciò, distruggendo anche il suo regno con l'acqua.

E sì, Noè fu la seconda volta che Dio distrusse la terra con l'acqua.

Potrebbe essere la ragione per cui lui (Satana) è sempre a creare problemi a noi, perché Dio lo ha detronizzato e ha distrutto il suo regno, e ha creato una nuova creazione per l'uomo, e questo regno ora appartiene all'uomo. Non dovete credere a me su questo, è solo cibo per il pensiero.

Spero e prego che questo libro vi spinga a cercare il Signore da soli. Iniziate la vostra relazione personale con Lui, siate originali proprio come Dio vi ha creati.

Vi auguro una giornata benedetta.

Appunti

44

Appunti

Appunti

46

Appunti

47

Appunti

Appunti

49

Appunti

Appunti

51

Appunti

Appunti

53

Appunti

Appunti

Sull'Autore:

Dopo aver subito abusi da bambino, Philip Guenaga ha superato queste terribili esperienze servendo per dieci anni nell'esercito e consegnando la sua vita a Dio quando aveva 17 anni. Attualmente è in pensione e svolge lavoro volontario presso un ospedale.

57

www.ingramcontent.com/pod-product-compliance
Lightning Source LLC
Chambersburg PA
CBHW032033040426
42449CB00007B/889